2009 Poetry Competition fo
YoungWriters

I have a dream 2009
Words to change the world

Martin Luther King

John Lennon

British Isles
Edited by Vivien Linton

First published in Great Britain in 2009 by:

Young Writers
Remus House
Coltsfoot Drive
Peterborough
PE2 9JX
Telephone: 01733 890066
Website: www.youngwriters.co.uk

All Rights Reserved
Book Design by Spencer Hart & Tim Christian
© Copyright Contributors 2009
SB ISBN 978-1-84924 393 3

Foreword

'I Have a Dream 2009' is a series of poetry collections written by 11 to 18-year-olds from schools and colleges across the UK and overseas. Pupils were invited to send us their poems using the theme 'I Have a Dream'. Selected entries range from dreams they've experienced to childhood fantasies of stardom and wealth, through inspirational poems of their dreams for a better future and of people who have influenced and inspired their lives.

The series is a snapshot of who and what inspires, influences and enthuses young adults of today. It shows an insight into their hopes, dreams and aspirations of the future and displays how their dreams are an escape from the pressures of today's modern life. Young Writers are proud to present this anthology, which is truly inspired and sure to be an inspiration to all who read it.

Contents

Biddulph High School, Stoke-on-Trent

Jonathan Senn (14) 1
Jasmin Manley (14) 2
Amber Foster (14) 3
Katie Alcock (14) 4
Lauren Whiteman (13) 5
John Hammond (13) 5
Kate Edwards (14) 6
Hannah Silverwood (14) 6
Bethany Eardley (13) 7
Chris Ryles (13) 7
Billy Horton (14) 8
Charlotte Garner (14) 9
Martha Brough (14) 10
Toni Holland (14) 10
James Shufflebotham (14) 11
Victoria Webb (13) 11

Cheadle Hulme High School, Cheadle Hulme

Lydia Oldfield (12) 12
Christian Beddows (11) 13
Jamie Hazelby (12) 14
Danielle Miller (11) 15
Sam Ward (13) 16
Jess Lee (12) 17
Phillip Heatley (12) 18
Jorja Lawrence-Levy (11) 18
Dan Hickman (11) 19
Ellie Kirkham (12) 19
Gaby McKeever (12) 20
Scott Dearnaley (11) 21
Emily Otley (12) 22
Ella Squelch (12) 23
Megan-Jayne Graham (12) 24
Nico Ryback (13) 25
Coralise Adam (12) 26
George Butler (11) 27

Christ the King College, Newport, Isle of Wight

Megan Anderson (13) 27
Sophie Simmonds (12) 28
Sherena Jackson (13) 29
Rebecca Clawson (13) 30
Ella Batten (13) 31
David Parsons (12) 32
Jack Stapeley (13) 32
Niall Martin (13) 33
Sam Fallick (12) 34
Anja Bennett (13) 35
Alex Burgess (13) 35
Helen Scivier (12) 36
Olivia Williams (13) 36

Hartford High School, Northwich

Clio Jackson (12) 37
Caitlin Butterworth (11) 38
Hannah Bryan (12) 38
Ellie Wilde (11) 39
Sam Ayres (12) 39
Heather Fawcett (12) 40
Nathan Grudzien (11) 40
Elora Peers (11) 41
Scott Yuen-Smith (12) 41
Bethany O'Hanlon (12) 42
Hannah Bratherton (12) 42
Eleanor Bass (12) 43
Joshua Gerrard (13) 43
Lee Proctor (13) 44
Matthew Gallimore (12) 44
Cameron Cooper (11) 45
Ines Donnelly (11) 45
Michael Donati (11) 46
Matthew Fleet (13) 46
Bethany Ayres (13) 47
Liam Browne (12) 47
Rajnie Uppal (12) 48
Tom Baker (13) 48
Rowena Hallam (11) 49

Alex Ankers (13) 49
Catherine Hayes (11) 50
Gareth Jones (11) 50
Bradley Taberner (11) 50
Kirsty Proudman (12) 51
George Notman (12) 51
Oliver Quinn (12) 51
Georgianna Hunt (12) 52
Jack Finney (12) 52
Emma Simpson (11) 52

Humberston Park School, Grimsby
Chelsea Roberts, Dominic
& Kelsey Culf 53
Alischa Dunstan 53
Jennifer Meredith 54
Ty Birkett 54

Lake Middle School, Lake,
Isle of Wight
Lauren Odell (13) 54
Lauren James (12) 55
Elle Garland (12) 56
Georgia Rostron (11) 57
Charlotte Dollery (11) 58
Katie Norsworthy (11) 59
Chloe Hadcroft (12) 60
Lucy Ellis (11) 61
Kirsten Taylor (12) 62
Holly Winwood (12) 63
Lauren Newland (12) 64
Georgia Bennett (12) 65
Tom Carter (13) 65
Donna Grady (13) 66
Louise Herbert (12) 66
Haydn Nigh (12) 67
Aaron James (13) 67
Amber Khan (13) 68
Elliott Edgington & Shaun Rockall (13)... 68
Amy Clarke (11) 69
Holly Beckley (11) 69
Phoebe Hein (12) 70
Charlie Wright (11) 70
Sophie Cusworth (12) 71
Danielle Taylor (12) 71

Katie Davis (13) 72
Toby Wilcock (13) 72
Meg Harper (11) 73
Samuel Durrant (12) 73
Jodie Hemming (13) 74
Sam Lancey (11) 74
Chloe Bird (12) 75
Anna Cole (11) 75
Millie Graham (11) 76
Billy Rose (12) 76
Courtney Sandison (13) 77
Paige Arnold (11) 77
Kieran Calvert (12) 78
Clara Murphy (11) 78
Chelsea Simpson (13) 79
Kane Fox (12) 79
Joshua Collings (13) 80
Connor Gray (12) 80
Blythe Ely (12) 81
Josh Clark (12) 81
Sophie Knight (13) 82
Ben Wraxton (11) 82
Katie Lear (12) 83
Harry Lovett (12) 83
Aaron Jacobs (11) 84
Ben Taplin (13) 84
Joanna Hewison (13) 85
Luke Sheard (13) 85
Jack Pattinson (13) 86
Dan Tibbett (12) 86
Jasmine Watt (11) 87
Danii Wells (12) 87
Hannah Barfoot (13) 88
Lewis Wood (11) 88
Ryan Heelan (12) 89
Daniel Barlow (12) 89
Leah Simpson (12) 90
Kyle Jones (11) 90
Ashleigh Jones (12) 91
Hayley Evans (11) 91
Charlotte Everist (12) 92
Jack Broadhead (12) 92
Amber Cook (12) 93
Lauren Sparrow (12) 93
Kyle Chessell (12) 94

Matthew Gibbon (11) 94
Mark Birch (13) 95
Nathan McCarthy (12) 95
Zoë Lane (11) 96
Katherine Turner (12) 96
Kimberley Wills (12) 97
Max Harris (11) 97
Brandon Hanmore (12) 98
Elliott Bell (13) 98
Maddie Hughes (12) 99
Sean Skinner (12) 99
Liam Seymour (12) 100
Charlie Abbott (11) 100
Ali Hooper (11) 101
Howard Brown (11) 101
Josh Redford (13) 102
Casey Brook-Henderson (12) 102
Riggs Hurrell (13) 102
Elias Whittington (11) 103
Adam Yates (12) 103
Brandon Wright (11) 103
Jade Goodwin (12) 104
Rebecca Greenslade (12) 104
Joshua Taplin (13) 104
Georgia Willshire (11) 105

Mossley Hollins High School, Mossley

Shannen Atkinson (12) 105
Nathan Gittens (13) 106
Alice Manning (13) 107
Evan McIlwaine (13) 108
Chloe Brierley (11) 109
Jessica Foreman (14) 110
Hannah Willis (14) 111
Lucy Mansfield (14) 112
Callum Leech (12) 112
Lauren Bishop (13) 113
Becky-Leigh Grimes (12) 114
Nia Woodhouse (12) 115
Philip Reynolds (11) 116
Jennifer Moloney (11) 116
Jack Shaw (11) & Daniel Parsons (12) .. 117
Emma Lowe 117
Charlie Barker (14) 118

Emily Lamb (14) 118
Charlotte Laycock (12) 119
Alexandra Kenworthy (12) 119
Mathilda Jackson-Hall (12) 120
Andrew Lawton (14) 120
Rachel Gaskell (12) 121
Sarah Lamb (11) 121
Adam Carter (11) 122
Shannon Connaghan (14) 122
Amy Pollitt (14) 123
Joshua Leah (11) 123
Rachel Hardiman (12) 124
Erin Barnes (12) 124
Emily Cassinelli (13) 125
Sarah Lowe (14) 125

Our Lady's RC High School, Oldham

Nicole Darrington (12) 126
Johnathan Hilton 127
Chloe Appleby 128
Isabella Smith (12) 129
Kristina Taylor 130
Angie Rodriguez Brady (14) 131
Ashlin Ellis (11) 132
Katie Dolotko (13) 133
Laura Marinelli 133
Abigail King (11) 134
Grace Stevenson 135
Sophie Lawton (13) 135
Nathan Calland-Storey (12) 136
Elizabeth Earnshaw (13) 136
Gemma Jackson (15) 137
Victoria Bacigalupo (12) 138
Megan Mitchell (13) 138
Amber Parker (13) 139
Georgie Walker 139
Michael Robson (14) 140
Molly Greaves (12) 140
Rebecca Harmer 141
Francesca Connolly (12) 141
Elise Robinson (13) 142
David Kelly (14) 142
Danny Gilbert (12) 143
Caitlin Shires 143

Jessica Burnett (12).............................. 143
Hannah Lowe 144
Luis Fay (13).. 144

Redland High School, Redland
Rebecca Glover (15) 145
Lauren Hall (11) & Anna Garcia (12) 146

St Katherine's School, Bristol
Adele Mitchell (13)................................ 147

Sir William Stanier Community High School, Crewe
Jessica Harper (13) 148
Aderayo Folorunso (14)......................... 149
Charlotte Ayers (13).............................. 150
Hollie Andrew (13) 150
Liam Astbury (12) 151
Leon Robinson & Jack Lightfoot........... 151

The Phoenix School, Fulbourn
Rosie Barratt (17) 152
Lizzie Hill (14)....................................... 153
Lisa Quick (16) 154

Thomas Keeble School, Stroud
Jack Smith (12)..................................... 155

Ventnor Middle School, Ventnor, Isle of Wight
Niall Mouat (12) 155
James Dymock (13)............................... 156
Cameron Guy (13)................................. 157
Connah Newton (12) 158
Chris Delaney (13)................................ 159
Jake Hitchcock (12)............................... 160
Luke Pestell (12)................................... 161
Josh Herridge (13)................................ 162
Cameron Lyons (12).............................. 163
Ahmet Suleyman (12)............................ 164
Caeden Cattell (12) 165
Alexander Conrad (13) 165
Jack Little (12) 166
George Atkey (12) 166
James Bott (13) 167
Tom Dawson (13) 168

Tom Redhead (12).................................. 169
Connor Jay Steptoe (13) 170

Western Study Plus Centre, Grimsby
Nikki Carter (15) 171

Withington Girls' School, Manchester
Esme Elsden (13).................................. 172
Véronique Tamin (16) 173
Sheanna Patel (13)............................... 174

The Poems

I Have A Dream - For All Those People Out There

I have a dream . . .
In my world everyone will live
In perfect peace and harmony,
Whether fat or thin, tall or small, black or white,
We could all learn to live together.

The disabled citizens of our racist world all have a vision,
A life which is fairer and a life without pain,
A life without prejudice.
The physical disabilities are most easy to spot,
But many people suffer alone in the dark,
Undiagnosed and looking for life.
Dyslexia and bipolar are all examples
For the hidden sufferers in our world,
Often misunderstood and thought of as scum,
But many people are just looking for love,
Someone to care, someone to love,
Someone to look out for them
In this harsh, harsh world.

Often thought of as the bane of society,
The 'idiot', the 'helpless',
The patronised few,
But we're about to revolt and make you all suffer
Like you did us for many, many years.
The only way to stop it is for you all to change,
Look inside your heart for all your good,
Believe in equality and it will believe in you.
Thank you.

Jonathan Senn (14)
Biddulph High School, Stoke-on-Trent

One Child's Dream

I went to sleep last night
With lots of thoughts in my head
About how the world should be,
With no one left unfed.

A world with no pollution
And no black, choking smog,
The ozone layer untouched
By this deadly, thick fog.

No rubbish on the roads,
No people on the street,
Who live in tiny boxes
And have nothing much to eat.

War and conflict rule the world,
When all we want is peace.
We need to stop our actions
And let the battles cease.

Many races roam the streets,
But some may get abuse.
We need to stop our racist words
And join to make a truce.

But I am just one concerned child,
Who no one will listen to.
I can't change the world all by myself,
I really need help from you.

Jasmin Manley (14)
Biddulph High School, Stoke-on-Trent

The Dream

I have a dream which is very small,
But in the future it could change us all.
Where we will live in a world of our own,
In this world we would care for every bird, tree, rock and stone.

There would be no pollution,
There would be a solution
For everything wrong that we've done.
We will start from where we began.

There would be no racism,
There would be no violence,
There would be nothing wrong,
We would all live together and get along.

In this world for you and me
There would be a deep blue, sparkling sea.
Flowers would grow in every field,
Our world would be protected by an invisible shield.

The animals in our world would be our friends, not food,
On this world there would be no such thing as a bad mood.
We would only use the things we need
And not use them up with all our greed.

This is my dream.

Amber Foster (14)
Biddulph High School, Stoke-on-Trent

There's Nothing That You Can Hide

There's nothing that you can hide,
Your colour,
Your style,
Your face,
Your race.
There's nothing that you can hide,
Your music,
Your braces,
Your flab,
Your bones.
There's nothing that you can hide,
You're poor,
You're posh,
You own lots of dosh,
The cash comes rolling in,
People don't understand that
Bullying isn't fun,
When your tears flow by
Like you've got nowhere to run.
Bullies are full of pain,
But confident on the outside.
But have a thought for the bully,
When his mum ignores him all night.

Katie Alcock (14)
Biddulph High School, Stoke-on-Trent

A Different Way Of Thinking

When I grow up I want to be a WAG,
Wear big shades and drive a Jag,
Go shopping all day, with my superstar friends,
Gucci, Chanel and all the latest trends.

I'll go to parties every night,
Then to LA, I'll get a flight,
To tan on the beach all day through
And get my nails done, what else is there to do?

But maybe this life isn't so great,
The nails, the hair, all so fake.
Maybe my friends won't like me for me,
They'll like the person I don't want to be.

I still want the money, the fortune, the fame,
And I want people to remember my name,
But because I got this through somebody else,
This in fact is not being myself.

A doctor, a lawyer is what I want to be,
So I can change the world and be the real me.
All I am saying is there are lots of ways to be seen,
So remember my name because I have a dream!

Lauren Whiteman (13)
Biddulph High School, Stoke-on-Trent

The Dream

I have a dream . . .
That there is no racism to see.
I have a dream . . .
That the world stays together in harmony,
No more hatred, no more fear,
No more hurt, no more tears,
This is what I want to see.
Finally I'm speaking up for the world, for me.

John Hammond (13)
Biddulph High School, Stoke-on-Trent

That's My Dream

I have a dream
Poverty and war will end,
We'll all have money to spend.
That's my dream!

I have a dream,
No racism anymore,
This I think should be the law.
That's my dream!

I have a dream,
No pollution to be seen,
This will make the Earth clean.
That's my dream!

I have a dream,
I know this will soon come true,
Because I believe and so should you.
That's my dream!

Kate Edwards (14)
Biddulph High School, Stoke-on-Trent

I Have A Dream

I have a dream
Of a harm-free life,
A life without a knife.

I have a dream
Where racism is no more,
And as for the disabled, a cure.

I have a dream.
My dream is for a pure world,
So let creation be unfurled.

Hannah Silverwood (14)
Biddulph High School, Stoke-on-Trent

I Have A Dream

I dream of a world
Where snow falls free,
Five months of the year
And anyone can ski.

I dream of a world
Where the other five months
The sun shines bright
Even in the slums.

I dream of a world
Where the remaining two months
The thunderstorms brew
I dream of a world.

The world would have
Snow, sun and sea
The world would be active
I dream of a world.

Bethany Eardley (13)
Biddulph High School, Stoke-on-Trent

Untitled

I have a dream, when I'm older and loaded,
I'll have so much money my wallet exploded.
Fountains of champagne, covered in gems,
A private penthouse overlooking the Thames.
Through this veil I see African children who cry,
Tumbledown shanty towns of those doomed to die.
I see all this poverty, my world tears at the seams,
My intent now is to stop this pain, these are my dreams.

Chris Ryles (13)
Biddulph High School, Stoke-on-Trent

I Have A Dream

I dream of a world without racism,
Where there are no racist idiots,
Where everybody is equal, no matter the colour of their skin.
I have a dream.

No war, no poverty and no difference,
We shall all be equal.
There shall be no difference.
I have a dream.

We treat our own race like the next,
We treat people with courtesy,
We treat everybody like our family.
I have a dream.

No love and no harmony in this world today,
Freedom of speech ends up in execution,
The people of this world will pay.
I have a dream.

Billy Horton (14)
Biddulph High School, Stoke-on-Trent

A Clean Tomorrow

I have a dream of magic powers,
Of a world that's yours and ours.
Although my dream is fairly small,
If we all dream, it helps us all.

Invisible me, invisible you,
But wait a minute, that's not true.
We're all people with a voice,
Together we can make a choice.

The choice should be to change our lives,
You may be in for a surprise.
Surprise is good and so is change,
So please try to convert your ways.

Recycle for a clean tomorrow,
Or live your life in pain and sorrow.
Please, just try to do your bit
And you could see a benefit . . .

Charlotte Garner (14)
Biddulph High School, Stoke-on-Trent

Go Unicorns!

I dream a dream . . .
Where unicorns frolic and play,
The trees stand still, undamaged,
Birds fly high, gliding through the sky,
Where nobody's hurt or harmed.

I dream a dream . . .
Where glitter shines like the sun,
The people live together in harmony,
Animals can roam free
And money isn't important.

I dream a dream . . .
Where everybody's treated the same,
When poverty doesn't exist,
When every person is happy and content.

I dream a dream . . .

Martha Brough (14)
Biddulph High School, Stoke-on-Trent

I Have A Dream . . .

I have a dream of dreaming,
Living in my mind,
Living in my own world,
Nothing bad you'll find.

I have a dream of dreaming,
Magic in the air,
Pixies, fairies, rainbows,
Nothing that would scare.

I have a dream of dreaming,
Love everything around,
In my dreams all is perfect,
Pretty, happy, sound.

Toni Holland (14)
Biddulph High School, Stoke-on-Trent

Dream

I have a dream,
A dream of equality,
The quality of equality,
A desperation for equality,
An earnestness for rights and reality,
Where Man lives harmoniously,
Away from the grasp of prejudice,
The harsh jaws of racism,
Should be closed forever,
The content of their mouths - banished,
Effects that these words take,
Mental infliction leading to insanity,
Originality and being unique,
That is the way Man struts . . .

James Shufflebotham (14)
Biddulph High School, Stoke-on-Trent

Dilemmas Of The World

When I grow up I want poverty to end,
I want everyone fed,
To have a nice cosy bed.
When I grow up I want poverty to end.

When I grow up I want child abuse to stop,
Kids not to feel threatened,
Always come first, never second.
When I grow up I want child abuse to stop.

When I grow up I want racism to end,
I want everyone to see the inside,
I don't want people to see the colour of the outside and judge.
When I grow up I want racism to end.

Victoria Webb (13)
Biddulph High School, Stoke-on-Trent

By The Time I Am Old . . .

By the time I am old,
I would like some things,
To find a pot of gold,
To fly without wings.

For there to be no wars,
No illness or pain
Lots of super new cures,
All happy again.

To swim the deepest seas,
To sprint the whole Earth,
To climb the big trees,
Show them what I'm worth.

To see every creature,
To meet everyone,
To be a dance teacher
And the greatest mum.

For us all to have fun,
And equal are we,
Us to love everyone,
And all still drink tea.

Pollution? There's none!
Recycle? It's great!
Doing it, everyone!
And *whooo,* no more hate.

I have missed some things out,
Like growing a seed,
Some things I want to shout,
But these things I need.

Lydia Oldfield (12)
Cheadle Hulme High School, Cheadle Hulme

I Have A Dream

I have a dream,
A dream of the future,
A dream that all shall be free,
That all shall not be poor, homeless or hungry,
That the slave trade will not exist.
I have a dream,
A dream of peace,
A dream of when war will be no more,
That all shall be happy,
That the terrorists live no more.
I have a dream
That in the future
We shall all live happily,
We shall have plenty to eat
And no animals will be endangered.
I have a dream
That in the future
We shall have explored hundreds of galaxies in outer space,
We shall all have high-tech skyscrapers,
And have discovered new species of animals.
I have a dream
That in the future
The Earth will flourish with plants and animals,
The Earth will have resolved its CO_2 problems,
And the Earth shall be restored to its original status.
I have a dream
That we will whizz around in hover cars,
That we shall be pleasant with each other
And that we shall all be happy again.
I have a dream . . .

Christian Beddows (11)
Cheadle Hulme High School, Cheadle Hulme

When I'm Older I'm Going To . . .

When I'm older I'm going to
Go out and find the biggest cure
The strongest cure
A cure that will destroy the horrible thing
A cure that can stop deaths
A cure that will make most people happy

When I'm older I'm going to be
A doctor that can save people
Stop those people dying
Help the people in need
Kill the disease
Fight the disease
Demolish the disease
Hate the disease

When I'm older I'm going to stop
The stupid nightmare
The thing that hurts people
Doesn't think about others
I'm going to cure cancer

When I'm older I'm going to sound strange
It's not going to be easy
But I'm sure going to fight and fight
Till I win
The disease can win against others
But with me it's like an ant
And it's just waiting to be squished by me
So when I grow up that's what I'm going to be.

Jamie Hazelby (12)
Cheadle Hulme High School, Cheadle Hulme

Bullying

Sometimes it feels like life is unfair,
Yet that is often when a bully is there.
When they pick and shout,
And smack and pout,
They never care.

The victim never deserves it at all,
They shrink and shrink until they're small.
Soon it feels like they will turn to dust,
Or get so hurt they'll burn and rust.
They can't take it.

Though sometimes the worst part of all
Is that it does not stop, not at all.
The teachers always hear them plead,
Yet the bullies continue with each deed,
The tears keep falling.

That is why I have a dream
To put an end to the cold and mean.
With the bullies finally gone,
Me, you and everyone
Can live in peace and harmony.

But it still feels like life is unfair,
Yet that is always when a bully is there.
They still pick and shout,
And smack and pout,
They won't ever care.

Danielle Miller (11)
Cheadle Hulme High School, Cheadle Hulme

The Right

We can rise up
Fight for justice
Righteousness, philosophy
Most of all
For the rights
Of any
Person

Any single human being
Must have the right
School, college, university
The right
To learn
By any means necessary

Any human being
Must have the right
Grow up, have a future
To become successful
To provide for themselves
Their family

We are all equal
In this world
And no matter what
Colour or nation we are
We are all one family
And one world.

Sam Ward (13)
Cheadle Hulme High School, Cheadle Hulme

I Have A Dream

I have a dream,
I have a dream that I share with millions of people,
I have a dream that many nations want to come true,
I have a dream that I believe will happen,
I have a dream that I know I will make happen.

Many people see the look in the doctor's face
when he tells them the bad news,
Many people go for all the treatment and fight it,
Many people lose hope and don't fight it,
Many people live and thank God every day
for pulling them through it,
Many more people don't.

One day my dream will come to life,
One day I will kill that vicious hook that comes down
from the sky to catch its next victims,
One day I will get revenge on the thing
That took my grandma, my uncle, my great grandad,
and so many more of my loving family away from me,
One day someone will stop the suffering of so many others,
One day I will stop the suffering of so many others.

I have a dream to cure cancer,
I have a dream that I will make reality.

Jess Lee (12)
Cheadle Hulme High School, Cheadle Hulme

I Had A Dream . . .

I had a dream
That I was hurtling towards the finish line
Metres ahead of Usain Bolt
With the wind in my face
The sound of the cheering in my ears
About to win the 200m sprint.

I had a dream
That I was gliding a Boeing 747 in to land
With buttons flashing all over the place
The runway seconds away
The brakes on full
At the biggest airport in the world.

I had a dream
That I was screeching around the inside of the last corner
Of the 2010 Formula 1 championship finals
On the final straight
Neck and neck with Lewis Hamilton
Chequered flag in sight.

But dreams don't really come true,
Or do they?

Phillip Heatley (12)
Cheadle Hulme High School, Cheadle Hulme

Everyone Has A Dream

Everyone has a dream,
Desires and ambitions,
Big or small, hold on to your dream.
Never aspire to be something you're not,
In spite of what everyone says,
As long as you remain determined,
You can achieve anything you want.

Jorja Lawrence-Levy (11)
Cheadle Hulme High School, Cheadle Hulme

I Have A Dream 2009 - British Isles

Living The Dream!

I want to live the dream . . .

By becoming an actor
And being on the TV,
Seeing my face in magazines
And on the cover of DVDs.

I want to be a billionaire
And drive the coolest cars.
I want to own everything,
From hotels down to bars.

I want to be the new James Bond
And be a sneaky spy.
I want to have the coolest gadgets
And watch the bad guys die.

I want this as my future,
To be the cast and crew,
So I'm going to try my hardest
To make my dream come true!

I want to live the dream . . .

Dan Hickman (11)
Cheadle Hulme High School, Cheadle Hulme

I Have A Dream . . .

I have a dream, to pursue or fulfil,
Where man or woman will not dream to kill.
A dream to not define them, her or him,
What does it matter, the colour your skin?
A dream to save those with a pitiful life,
Take them away from streets of strife.
A dream to keep the world peaceful and pure,
Stop the Earth's eternal war . . .

I have a dream . . .

Ellie Kirkham (12)
Cheadle Hulme High School, Cheadle Hulme

I Had A Dream

I had a dream,
It was the biggest day of my life.
I was about to begin the match
That would decide who was going to win.
As we lined up on the pitch,
Before we'd even started,
We had a group huddle,
But when the whistle blew, we parted.
We started with the ball
Then we went into a maul.
'Oh yes, come on,' he scored a try.
The other team's manager
Was still shouting, 'Why?'
The whistle blew as the ball
Went out the back line,
England had won for the seventh time.
As we raised the cup with glee,
All the fans shouted, *'Yippee!'*
The man of the match was Johnny - of course,
And everyone gave him a big round of applause.

Gaby McKeever (12)
Cheadle Hulme High School, Cheadle Hulme

I Have A Dream

I have a dream that life shall last all eternity.
I have a dream that animals shall never change.
Dogs shall always bark,
Cats shall always miaow,
Birds shall always fly,
Fish shall always swim.
I have a dream that life shall last all eternity.
As long as I live, mankind shall never upgrade,
The oceans and seas shall never dry,
Forests will never be lifeless,
Deserts shall never be wet.
I have a dream that life shall last all eternity.
Creatures shall always change,
Seeds shall always grow to flowers,
Caterpillars shall always change to butterflies,
Tadpoles shall always change to frogs.
I have a dream that life shall last all eternity.
Planet Earth shall never be as hot as Mars
Or as cold as Pluto,
But shall always be home to life.

Scott Dearnaley (11)
Cheadle Hulme High School, Cheadle Hulme

I Have A Dream

I have a dream
What dream?
A lovely dream.
A little dream for now
That could become a big dream.

Do you have a dream?
No?
I don't believe that they come true
What could my dream be?
Listen to me and you might see . . .

I dream that we live in a world
Where people give instead of wanting to be given.

I dream that we live in a world
Where every corner we turn there is happiness.

I dream that people will dream
They may not always come true
But if you try, there's no harm you can do.

Emily Otley (12)
Cheadle Hulme High School, Cheadle Hulme

I Have A Dream

When the future comes,
I will be gone,
So here's a message
For my loved one.

Make sure everyone is happy,
Having fun.
Make sure that poverty
Has not won.

When times get rough
It may feel like everything's bad,
But try and put on a smile,
Then I'll be glad.

And when the future comes,
You will be gone,
So leave this message
For your loved one.

Ella Squelch (12)
Cheadle Hulme High School, Cheadle Hulme

My Dream

I have a dream
Not to be rich
Or to be famous.
I don't care
About make-up
Or the latest fashions,
The latest gadgets
Or music in the charts.
My dream . . .
To solve world hunger
Or to shelter the homeless.
My dream . . .
To love the lonely
Or make peace on Earth.
My dream . . .
To answer the unanswered
Or to find the unfound?

Megan-Jayne Graham (12)
Cheadle Hulme High School, Cheadle Hulme

Our Dream

We all have a dream,
The one thing we stick by
For the rest of our life.
My dream is to be a solicitor,
Bring justice to our cruel world.

We all have a dream.
We *will* bring justice to this world
If we work together we can
Make this world a better place.
Let's listen to the law.

We all have a dream
This world will be a better place.
We must bring justice to this world.
All we have to do is work together.

We all have a dream.

Nico Ryback (13)
Cheadle Hulme High School, Cheadle Hulme

The Betting Of Dreams

I bet fifty that my dreams are better than yours
I dream of dragons and sometimes swords
What do you bet that your dreams are better than mine?
Oh sorry, I forgot you use dimes
I dream of everything like skiing down mountains
Playing in fountains and stuff like that
I bet that your dreams are boring, not exciting
You just sit while I'm the one fighting
With disgusting scary monsters, dragons and beasts
I beat them all and have yummy feasts
I dream of butterflies, pink flowers in a row
Wings of gold take me to a rainbow
You just sit sadly doing nothing in the rain
You're the one whose heart is bleeding with pain
All you have to do is imagine and believe
And I bet you could join me in my dream.

Coralise Adam (12)
Cheadle Hulme High School, Cheadle Hulme

I Have A Dream

One man, fuelled by passion for his great dream,
Going on a quest for all that is right.
His task, impossible as it may seem,
Is unity of people, black and white.
A world without segregation and rank,
Where all are equal and none mistreated.
Out of all in the world, he is to thank,
The one man, whom at that time, was hated.
His idea was right, but none agreed,
He continued with his difficult thought,
But now succeeding with increasing speed.
He gradually gained the trust of the court.
He, the one who changed the world we live in,
Now dead but honoured, Martin Luther King.

George Butler (11)
Cheadle Hulme High School, Cheadle Hulme

Knife Crime

Violence
Is everywhere in our streets.
Death
Is making us feel incomplete.
Happy
Is a word that people have forgotten,

Knife crime has to stop!

Safe
Is how children should feel.
Love
Is true, it helps us heal.
Together
Is a feeling being torn apart,

Knife crime, it leaves a hole in our heart.

Megan Anderson (13)
Christ the King College, Newport, Isle of Wight

Cruelty

Do you really like it?
Is it really worth it?
What if it was you?
Is it worth the pain?

Shouldn't you just stop it?
Make it easier for them
Because it isn't really worth it,
The guilt from you
And the pain from them.

Animals really matter -
More than some may think.
We're worth all the same,
So try to find the link.

Let's kick sense into the people
Who think that they are right.
You won't and can't get away with it -
Will you get in trouble?
You might.

So stop abusing animals,
Because it really isn't fair;
There's no good excuse or good opinion,
Because to be honest, no one cares.

If we put an end to cruelty
And take the benefit of the doubt,
It's certain the world would be happier
If we don't hear the animals shout.

Sophie Simmonds (12)
Christ the King College, Newport, Isle of Wight

Imagine A World

Imagine a world of harmony,
Peace and trust in one another,
Without disparity, discrimination or racism.
Imagine a world where the heart
Overflows with kindness and modesty.
Imagine a world where every human being
Is being treated with respect that they deserve,
Without discrimination or taking advantage
Of vulnerable people, no matter how old they may be,
The colour of their skin, their origin.
Everyone on this planet is to be treated equally.
Imagine a world where smiles surround
Every cheerful face and light up an unhappy face.
Imagine a world of prosperity and cheerfulness
That fills the whole nation.
Imagine a world where people can go out of their homes
Not being afraid of leaving their door open.
Imagine a world where trust is at
The essence of every being of the human race.
A world of love shared from person to person.
Imagine a world full of warmth where every
Cold, negative heart is made a warm, loving one.
Imagine a world where the vicious discriminators and racists
Realise the true meaning of life
To love and share with one another.
Imagine what it would be like to live in this nation,
Full of harmony, kindness, prosperity and trust.
What a different place the world would be to live in.

Sherena Jackson (13)
Christ the King College, Newport, Isle of Wight

Child Cruelty

Children are children,
Not victims.
Children are children,
Not targets.

You were a child,
Not a victim.
You were a child,
Not a target.

No one should fear
Tomorrow.
No one should fear
Their parents.

No one should have
Cuts and bruises.
No one should have
No friends.

Do you think
They want pain?
Do you think
They want suffering?

Stop. Now.

Rebecca Clawson (13)
Christ the King College, Newport, Isle of Wight

Imagine . . .

Imagine a world without poverty,
Death, hunger and cruelty.
Imagine a world where no one gets hurt:
That is the world for me!

Imagine a world without poverty,
Pain, famine and slavery.
Imagine a world full of smiles:
That is the world for you!

Imagine a world without poverty,
Drugs, murder and adultery.
Imagine a world careless and free:
That is the world for me!

Innocent children are victims,
Mothers are anxious and sick.
Fathers go out and waste money:
It needs to be stopped, *quick!*

I have a dream that we will all be happy,
Relaxed and carefree.
No one will worry or have to be sorry:
That is the world for everybody!

Ella Batten (13)
Christ the King College, Newport, Isle of Wight

Animal Testing

Rats are captured and taken to a laboratory,
They wee in cages and have no lavatory.
Then they're taken out to test shampoo,
I'm sure they really don't want to.

Rabbits are taken, dwarves, French, Dutch,
And trussed up in a really tiny hutch.
Do they want to be in this mess?
I'm sure you can make a guess.

Guinea pigs are scared, really, really frightened
When they're put on a table with straps tighter than tightened.
They're forced to take medicine, sometimes even eye drops,
And if it goes badly, one of their eyes pops!

Mice are caught and barely fed,
Most of them end up dead.
They test medicines, antibiotics too,
They die for the benefit of you!

David Parsons (12)
Christ the King College, Newport, Isle of Wight

Child Abuse

Daddy, Daddy, please stop!
Daddy, Daddy, it hurts!
Daddy, Daddy, why?

I sit by the fire
But I'm cold.
I eat some food
But I'm still hungry.

Mummy, Mummy, what have I done?
Mummy, Mummy, please not again.
Mummy, Mummy, why?

What does love feel like?

Jack Stapeley (13)
Christ the King College, Newport, Isle of Wight

Racism

The world has been full of racism
Since the time of slavery,
I thank the Lord although I'm black
No one is racist to me.

'I have a dream,' Martin Luther said,
But some people weren't that chilled,
And Luther, on his balcony
That night, was horribly killed.

Racism is a terrible thing,
To separate white and black,
And all I want to say is this,
Why do racists need to attack?

If all races of humankind
Were to join their hands and pray,
Then I'm fully convinced that the Lord will smile
And all will be OK.

Niall Martin (13)
Christ the King College, Newport, Isle of Wight

Think About Poverty

Think about poverty,
It could be you or me.
Their lives could be positive,
If we could just give.

Why are people rich
And others poor?
We can't go on
With this anymore.

Think about poverty,
It will go on for eternity.
There's so much injustice,
We have to stop this.

Our sins are unforgivable.
Why are we so cruel?
We turn a blind eye to reality,
But together we *can* stop poverty.

Sam Fallick (12)
Christ the King College, Newport, Isle of Wight

Pollution

Pollution is now.
Litter, oil, filth and dirt.
Pollution is now!

Pollution can stop.
A clean, pure world full of peace.
Pollution can stop!

Pollution extinct.
Happy, smiley faces, *hooray!*
Pollution extinct!

Now I have a dream.
Pollution has to end now!
Now I have a dream!

Fulfilling my dream,
That is what must happen.
Fulfil this dream now!

Anja Bennett (13)
Christ the King College, Newport, Isle of Wight

Gang Culture

Gang culture is violent.
Gang culture is bullying.
Gang culture is vandalising our streets.
Gang culture rapes the citizens around us.
This *isn't* the world I want!
Now . . . I have a dream.
Longer jail sentences . . . Yes, that would help.
Keep youths occupied . . . Good!
Look out for everyone . . . See something?
Violence should be controlled . . . It's scary.
Rape? Rape? Rape? Rape? . . . No one deserves it.
Stop now!
This is my world just as much as yours.

Alex Burgess (13)
Christ the King College, Newport, Isle of Wight

Global Warming

Take a look at the world around us!
Lush forests, creatures sustaining each other,
Clean, sparkling waters, teeming with fish,
Birds, bees and butterflies playing their part,
Then Man becomes powerful . . .

Take a look at the world around us!
Man's new inventions tame the planet,
Our carbon footprints are growing fast,
Ocean rising whilst ice caps are melting,
Forests burning and habitats shrinking!

Take a look at the world around us!
One endless, parched desert,
No plants, no animals, no humans, no life!
An out of control world!
Can we prevent it?

Helen Scivier (12)
Christ the King College, Newport, Isle of Wight

Wounded Fields

A new beginning these people only dream of,
A lost emotion, a dying dream,
Soldiers must stare at a broken-hearted sky,
Traced with the outline of the bravest blood.

Later these soldiers lie on wounded fields,
Barely living, not always dead,
It's not always easy to trudge through knee-high mud,
When the mud is a part of your greatest friend.

Should you fight when there is need for talk?
What is a victory when all your friends are dead?
Look for understanding and not for advantage,
When wounded fields are mended, our children's to tend!

Olivia Williams (13)
Christ the King College, Newport, Isle of Wight

Writing

I love to write
In pen and on a lined pad,
Letting my mind run mad
For hours on end,
Driving me round the bend.
Hundreds of stories all over the place
I have a grin all over my face.
In the starlit sky
I read my stories
Till my mind runs dry.
All night,
All day,
Getting more ideas to write.
I was inspired
By books
And like to have a couple of crooks,
Scary, funny, happy, sad,
I have filled up my pad.
I want to write
Till I can't any more,
Or I'm a granny
And everyone knows me
For the famous person I was
And still am.
I need to write
And can never stop,
Unless I explode with a pop.
I get a good pay
And everyone likes me, I must say.
In pen and pad
I love to write
Till my mind runs mad.

Clio Jackson (12)
Hartford High School, Northwich

Inspiration

Inspiration is something special,
As special as can be,
Everyone has a voice to be heard in the crowd,
You need me as I need you,
Make friends,
Keep friends,
Have friends and love friends,
Make a world of your own,
Have a laugh,
Be good, be strong,
Do it now, before it's too late!

Don't give up now,
Inspire people, help people,
And move on,
Life is for living,
Life is for giving
But when hatred grows,
It grows like a weed,
Entwining and spinning,
Until it's nothing more than black,
So don't fade and hide away,
Be big and bright:
Live your life!

Caitlin Butterworth (11)
Hartford High School, Northwich

Inspiration

You are my hero,
My twinkling star,
When I feel the temptation to be bleak,
You have the guidance that I seek.
You say 'goodbye temptation',
That's why *you* are my inspiration!

Hannah Bryan (12)
Hartford High School, Northwich

Be Inspired

Be inspired with the light of day,
Things happen in the world.
Make them stop, so believe in life
That miracles do happen, so does peace.
Believe you're special and not dumb.

Inspiration is something special,
It comes from your heart,
So believe in peace and wonder
And then I will believe.
Make your dreams and live your dreams
And then they will come true.
Don't have problems, live your life.

Be inspired by what happens in life,
Like your parents, sisters, brothers,
Cousins, uncles, aunties and grandparents.
These people are special and they care for you,
So . . .

Don't think no one cares for you
Because we do and that's a fact,
And we only do because we are
Inspired with what happens in life.

Ellie Wilde (11)
Hartford High School, Northwich

Joe C

Joe Calzaghe, he's the best,
He'll take out any pest.
As cool as a fridge,
An exceptional fighter,
He burns like a lighter.
Stings with a punch,
He'll have anyone for lunch!

Sam Ayres (12)
Hartford High School, Northwich

Inspiration

If you think real hard,
What do you want to be?
If you sleep real deep,
What do you dream?
Who do you see
In your mind's eye
As a friend or inspiration?

Can inspiration be
A friend or foe?
Can it be trusted
Like family and friends?
What's inspiration to you?

Can inspiration
Be trusted or not?
Is it the enemy
To fire at?
What's inspiration to you?

If you think real hard
And sleep real deep,
What's inspiration to you?

Heather Fawcett (12)
Hartford High School, Northwich

Finnly

I have a dog, his name is Finn,
He stayed in Ireland in an inn.
He woofed at everyone going by,
So to shut him up I gave him my pie.

Finn is very, very clever,
He can sit down, roll around, and even pull a lever.
No one wanted him as a pup because he had brown on his leg,
But when we saw him everyone kissed him on the head.

Nathan Grudzien (11)
Hartford High School, Northwich

Imagine?

Imagine your idol,
Are they as good as this?
An idol willing to help,
To give, to be a friend?
An idol to do something dangerous
To save you from horror and Hell?
An idol, to be or not to be?
That is my question,
The answer is yours . . .

Imagine yourself as an idol,
Are you as good as this?
An idol willing to help,
To give, to be a friend?
An idol to do something dangerous
To save someone from horror and Hell?
An idol, to be great or not to be great?
That is my question,
The answer is yours . . .

Elora Peers (11)
Hartford High School, Northwich

Inspiration

I am inspired by people I like, but
N ot people I don't like
S uper he is
P roud to be himself
I nspiration to all
R eally fast
A person to be proud to be
T he love for the game
I n the game
O n TV
N ational great.

Scott Yuen-Smith (12)
Hartford High School, Northwich

Walking Through A World

Walking through a world,
It is in your hands,
But can slip away just like sand.

Feeling alone,
Since you have nothing to own.
Never give up because you are the best,
Since you don't have to be like the rest.

You have the making of,
Not doing the breaking,
Because you are who you want to be.

Imagine living your dream
And being who you seem,
The best you can be
For everyone to see.

Bethany O'Hanlon (12)
Hartford High School, Northwich

Inspiring

As long as you try hard enough,
You can be who you want to be.
Whether it's sport, dance, singing or happiness,
You can achieve it all by being inspired.

Work hard and play hard, never give up.
Ellen Whitaker inspires me
And so does Pippa Funnell.
They're both amazing riders
And I learn things from them both.

I watch them on television,
Praying for them to win
In competitions in which they ride,
It makes my mind spin.

Hannah Bratherton (12)
Hartford High School, Northwich

Follow Your Dreams

Winners never quit,
Quitters never win.
Winners always succeed,
Inspiration's all we need.

Who we believe in
Is who inspires us.
Family, friends, whatever,
It doesn't matter because . . .

Inspiration helps us follow our dreams,
No matter how hard it ever seems.

We follow the path that suits us best,
Because we don't have to follow the rest.
All you have to do is live your dreams through,
So you know that's the right path for you.

Eleanor Bass (12)
Hartford High School, Northwich

Lewis Hamilton

L eaves the track with a trophy
E nds the race first place
W ins often
I ndependent
S o fast

H as a fast car
A wesome at driving
M anages not to crash
I mmense at overtaking
L oves to drive
T akes the lead
O vertakes everybody
N ever stops.

Joshua Gerrard (13)
Hartford High School, Northwich

Inspired

I'm inspired by Usain Bolt
Because he's very fast,
He will never finish last.

I'm inspired by Usain Bolt,
Because he never gives up
And will always look up.

I'm inspired by Usain Bolt,
Because the faster, the stronger,
The race will be no longer.

I'm inspired by Usain Bolt,
Because he has a dream
To become the best.

Lee Proctor (13)
Hartford High School, Northwich

Usain Bolt

Usain Bolt, Usain Bolt,
What a man, not a single fault.
Starts the race, fears no pressure,
Finishes it and wins with pleasure.

Gets the record, he's the best,
Celebrates halfway in front of the rest.
What a man, what a star,
Even better than my grandpa.

Runs for his country, owns his dream,
He's amazing, the best in the team.
He's a man, he's a lad,
When he runs, I think he's mad.

Matthew Gallimore (12)
Hartford High School, Northwich

My Inspiration

Rafa Nadal inspires me,
I want to be just like him,
Playing tennis all day long,
Hitting forehands and backhands,
Hitting volleys and smashes.

Beating all the world's best players
And winning Wimbledon,
Getting loads and loads of cash,
Having a nice house and cars.

Move to Majorca,
Liking the dream,
And having loads of girls.

Cameron Cooper (11)
Hartford High School, Northwich

Inspire

Imagine someone near you,
Someone to look out for you,
Someone to care for you,
Someone from your family.

It could be your mum,
It could be your dad,
Whoever it is,
They should inspire you.

But why do they inspire you?
Are they living and caring?
Are they always positive?
Are they always there for you?

Ines Donnelly (11)
Hartford High School, Northwich

Redwall Daylight

Dawn and daylight bleach,
Illuminating the beach,
Glinting off the sandstone wall,
May Redwall Abbey never fall.
Stood tall and proud in Mossflower Woods,
Peace can reign but sometimes not.
The warrior of Redwall is the one
Who bears the sword which is his,
Protecting the abbey from whomever may attack.
He always has courage for everyone to see.
If you want a fight come and see me,
I am found on a tapestry.

Michael Donati (11)
Hartford High School, Northwich

Inspiration

People who inspire
Have got what they desire
They create their own spotlight
Which gives people certain delight
They have reached their goal
Because they have followed their soul
You can reach your dream
It would seem
Just listen to the voice inside your head
And you will desire
And one day you will inspire.

Matthew Fleet (13)
Hartford High School, Northwich

Inspiration

I am inspired by a person who
N ever does wrong in my eyes, who is
S pecial,
P retty and
I ntelligent too, she is
R eally inspirational
A nd
T houghtful
I n everything she does, she seizes every
O pportunity and
N ever gives up.

Bethany Ayres (13)
Hartford High School, Northwich

Lewis Hamilton

Lewis Hamilton, he's got his dream,
When he drives he makes me scream.
Starts the race with loads of pressure,
Finishes it and wins with pleasure.

He's a man, just a lad,
When he drives I think he's mad.
He's the best driver ever,
He doesn't even lose, not ever.

This is my poem, it's the end.
I wonder how fast he goes round the bend?

Liam Browne (12)
Hartford High School, Northwich

I Have A Dream

Do I have a dream, a sweet, sweet dream?
Maybe it's to meet the Queen.

Do I have an inspiration?
Full of determination,
Maybe yes, maybe no,
But I don't actually know.

Is my dream to sail the seas
Or to be a waiter making cups of tea?
All these questions I do not know the answer to,
Sorry to waste your time, but I don't have a clue.

Rajnie Uppal (12)
Hartford High School, Northwich

Inspired

Have you ever been inspired
To be who you are today?
Well, I have!
My uncle is an inspiration to me,
The way he puts his life on the line,
Being confident and fighting on
And for his country, not knowing
What might happen.
He gives me hope for me and my country,
The freedom we will always have.

Tom Baker (13)
Hartford High School, Northwich

My Teacher, Mr Lee

My teacher, Mr Lee,
Isn't horrible like a bumblebee,
He got hip, he got hop,
Now let's all do the bop.
He's like my best mate
And I see him through the school gate.
My teacher, Mr Lee,
Wish he came round for a cup of tea.
He is fun, fun as can be,
But don't be jealous, he's better than me.

Rowena Hallam (11)
Hartford High School, Northwich

Be Inspired

To inspire people can change the world.
Words can change the world.
All they need is to be spoken.

Being inspired will change the world,
It will create a hard-working world,
As someone shall want to be like someone else.

So try to inspire.
If you have a dream, let that dream come true.
All you need to do is not give up!

Alex Ankers (13)
Hartford High School, Northwich

I Will Never Give Up

I will never give up,
I will fight till the day I die.

I will never give up,
But I will fight with words and not my fists.

I will never give up,
Even if I fall down and cry.

I will never give up,
Even if I am just playing a game of hit and miss.

Catherine Hayes (11)
Hartford High School, Northwich

English Soldiers

English soldiers are great,
They all have a certain fate.
Going here, going there,
Making sides really fair.
Going out, helping men,
While they are dying in a medical den.
This is why I picked this subject,
Because they are given a mission
They will never object.

Gareth Jones (11)
Hartford High School, Northwich

Steven Gerrard

Stevie Gerrard, Gerrard,
He can hit a ball forty yards.
He's tough and he's proper hard,
I said Stevie Gerrard, Gerrard.

Bradley Taberner (11)
Hartford High School, Northwich

I Have A Dream

My favourite teacher is Miss Shewan,
We do a lot of sticking and gluing,
She is so fantastic and so great,
She is never really bothered when we are late.

My other favourite teacher is Mr Lee,
He is always buzzing around like a buzzy, buzzy bee.
He is so cool, better than me,
That's why he is Mr Lee.

Kirsty Proudman (12)
Hartford High School, Northwich

I Have A Dream

William Marsh, he's immense.
I look at him
And he's so dense.
He's as solid as a rock,
And as sound as a pound,
Best of all,
We're mates all around.

George Notman (12)
Hartford High School, Northwich

Inspiration

P eople can inspire you to do anything
E veryone can inspire you
O pportunities are everywhere, which are there for you
P eople you believe in will believe in you
L ove can inspire you
E ven in your dreams and everywhere.

Oliver Quinn (12)
Hartford High School, Northwich

I Have A Dream

Johanne, Johanne, she's so great,
That's why we are the best of mates.
We laugh and dance
And sing and play,
I can count on her every day!

Georgianna Hunt (12)
Hartford High School, Northwich

What Is Inspiration?

Inspiration is being inspired by someone.
Inspiration is inspiring someone.
Inspiration is wanting to be like someone.
Inspiration is . . .

Jack Finney (12)
Hartford High School, Northwich

I Have A Dream

Michael Morpurgo is completely insane,
He wrote a book 'Why the Whales Came'.
It's all about a birdman who is in pain,
Michael Morpurgo is completely insane.

Emma Simpson (11)
Hartford High School, Northwich

Our Dreams

As I lay in bed
Dreams in my head,
Who shall I be tonight?

A pirate on an adventure,
Looking for treasure?
A princess in a gleaming white dress,
Marrying her handsome prince?

A superhero flying around the world
Saving people from danger!
A basketball player shooting hoops,
1, 2, 3, that's me!

Not all of my dreams are happy ones,
Sometimes they can be scary,
When ghosts chase me and monsters shout *boo!*

Now the night has gone
And the moon takes my dreams away.
It's time to get out of bed and play.

Chelsea Roberts, Dominic & Kelsey Culf
Humberston Park School, Grimsby

My Dream To Be An Artist

One day I want to be an artist,
Using all the colours under the sun,
Making models, drawings and paintings,
Find it all really fun.
I will hang my paintings on the wall
So that they can be seen by all.

Alischa Dunstan
Humberston Park School, Grimsby

I Have A Dream

I have a dream
That one day I will become a baker
To make cakes filled with cream,
For Westlife and Beckham.
I want to be the best bread maker.

Jennifer Meredith
Humberston Park School, Grimsby

I Want To Be A Builder

I want to build houses and parks,
And skyscrapers and football stadiums.
These are big and are the best,
But I'd still enjoy building the rest.

Ty Birkett
Humberston Park School, Grimsby

Difference! Does It Involve Seal?

Difference!
What does it mean?
Managing feelings?
No
Empathy?
No
Social skills?
No
Motivation?
No
Self awareness?
Maybe
Difference!
What does it mean?

Lauren Odell (13)
Lake Middle School, Lake, Isle of Wight

I Have A Dream

I have a dream
To change what I have seen
To stop the drugs
Or even smoking.

Abuse in families
Is just not right
I don't see why
They should have sleepless nights.

They try to teach them to fight
The kids don't want to learn
So the dad says,
'Fine, your friend will burn.'

I know I hate them
But I can't frustrate them
Or they will hurt me more
But I can't tell the police what I saw.

Also there was the smoke
They were always rolling dope
They had this green stuff in their hand
Then they crushed it like sand.

Their eyes went really weird
I looked and said it was just to make me fear
But then I got scared,
They shouted at me for eating
They kept me in my room.

So one day I ran
And took the green stuff with me
They sounded mad in the morning
So I ran for my life
Then I saw posters

And on the telly they sounded sad
So I went back
They were rid of the stuff.

Lauren James (12)
Lake Middle School, Lake, Isle of Wight

Peer Pressure

Peer pressure,
Peer pressure,

Haunting every step I take,
Bullying me,
Pulling me,
Giving me something fake.

Peer pressure,
Peer pressure,

Making me steal from my dad,
I say no!
They're laughing
And they still think they're bad.

Peer pressure,
Peer pressure,

Saying no is hard,
But who do you tell?
You carry on with life,
However, it's just turning to hell.

Peer pressure,
Peer pressure,

My face is like a fiery sun,
They've punched me till I'm blue,
Bloody, blood dripping,
Two marbles closed tight.

Peer pressure,
Peer pressure,

Rivers stream down my cold cheeks,
Everything broken,
Including my heart,
I just feel hopeless.

Peer pressure,
Peer pressure,

The group is laughing still,
I'm choking madly,

'This is it!' I blast,
'I'm through being pressured
And through being bullied!'
I told someone and it stopped before I knew it.

Peer pressure,
Peer pressure,

If you are suffering this too
And you want to get through it,
Tell someone.

Peer pressure,
Peer pressure,
Peer pressure.

Elle Garland (12)
Lake Middle School, Lake, Isle of Wight

It's Them Against Me!

Why does it have to be me
That gets beaten for looking different
And called names for not being the same?
Being myself,
I can't help it, it's just who I am!

I try to stay away
But they keep on finding me.
I'm scared to go to school
In case they're there.
I want to tell someone,
But think, *what will they do?*

When will this stop?
I hope it is soon.

I have no friends because I get bullied,
They think the bullies might bully them.
I need to do something about this,
I need to make this *stop!*

Georgia Rostron (11)
Lake Middle School, Lake, Isle of Wight

57

Dreams

He had a dream,
I have a dream,
He dreamed that his four little children
Would not be judged by the colour of their skin, but by
                                    their character,
I have a dream that there will be no violence, no crime,
His dream came true,
Will mine?

He had a dream,
I have a dream,
He dreamed that black and white people
Would be able to join hands and love each other.
I have a dream that people will treat everyone kindly,
His dream made people think and change their minds,
Will mine?

He had a dream,
I have a dream,
He dreamed that there would be no more black slaves,
No more treating people differently because of the colour of their skin,
I have a dream that animals will never be mistreated,
His dream saved many from always being hurt physically and mentally,
Will mine?

He dreamed and dreamed,
I'm dreaming and dreaming,
Day and night,
Night and day,
He changed the world,
Will I?

All his dreams came true,
Will mine?

Will mine?

Charlotte Dollery (11)
Lake Middle School, Lake, Isle of Wight

I Have A Dream

I have a dream,
A dream for the world,
That my children will grow up to a planet,
That is full of peace.
I have a dream,
A dream for the world.

I have a dream,
A dream for the world,
That there will be no more injured soldiers,
The brave people who go out to save our country,
And don't return home, will be spared.
I have a dream,
A dream for the world.

I have a dream,
A dream for the world,
That there will be no more wars.
I have a dream,
A dream for this world.

I have a dream,
A dream for me,
That one day,
I will bring relief to suffering animals.
I have a dream,
A dream for me.

I have a dream,
A dream for me,
That I will make ill animals healthy again,
A dream that one day I will be a vet.
I have a dream,
A dream for me.

Katie Norsworthy (11)
Lake Middle School, Lake, Isle of Wight

Abuse

Tears wept on the velvet sheets
As blood swept the deserted streets
People ask but you don't like to tell
You always say you used to fall
You wonder if you should ever tell

Broken nose
Smacked in the face
Bloody lip
He is such a disgrace
Sometimes you want to smack him in the face

My life got brighter
No more smacks in the face
I love my kids
They see the scar on my face
They ask me what happened to my face
I always say, 'Your daddy hit me in the face
He is a disgrace.'

I love my life
It's as good as can be
I see my kids smile at me
It makes me feel happy about me
Thank God for saving me
I'm glad I stopped this terrible pain

My mum, my dad, my Ally
Are here to look after me
I respect them and love them
With all of my heart
And never will leave them
Till death will us part.

Chloe Hadcroft (12)
Lake Middle School, Lake, Isle of Wight

Child Abuse

Tears streaming down their faces,
Parents shouting,
It should stop.

Hitting and punching,
A new bruise every day,
It should stop.

Running to their rooms,
Too scared to come out,
It needs to stop.

Screaming as Mum,
Gives you a black eye,
It needs to stop.

Too scared to stand up to the bully,
That is your own mother,
It could stop.

Pretend that you're clumsy
And not beaten up,
It could stop.

Scars all over your body,
That you never want to show,
It may stop.

You go to bed with a bleeding nose,
And you never want to wake up.
It may stop.

Child abuse is horrid,
Tell someone you can trust,
It will stop!

Lucy Ellis (11)
Lake Middle School, Lake, Isle of Wight

My Dream World

I dream I could meet some of my idols.
                              Idols.
I dream I could act with some of my idols.
                              Act with my idols.
I dream there is no more homework.
                              Homework.
I dream everyone could have magic powers.
                              Powers.
I dream there is peace everywhere.
                              Everywhere.
I dream we could teleport anywhere we want to.
                              Want to.
I dream that climate change can be reduced to a small amount.
                              Amount.
I dream I could be powerful.
                              Powerful.
I dream I can stay friends with the ones I know now.
                              Know now.
I dream that no more female or male children will get abused.
                              Abused.
I dream no more pets will get hurt anymore.
                              Anymore.
I dream I could have a million pounds to spend.
                              Spend.
I dream I could be more healthy.
                              Healthy.
I dream this place can be a better place.
                              Place.
These are my dreams, do you have one?

Kirsten Taylor (12)
Lake Middle School, Lake, Isle of Wight

Run, Run, Run, Run

Run, run, run, run,
He's catching up with me,
Like a tiger hunting its prey,
He'll get me, you'll see.

Run, run, run, run,
I really have to stop,
I'm getting short of breath,
I think I'm gonna drop.

Run, run, run, run,
I need to get away,
Oh no, he's getting faster,
This might be my last day.

Trip, fall, skid, stop,
He's towering over me now,
If I don't get up then,
Please no, *ow!*

Cry, cry, cry, cry,
Crushing me with his huge paw,
Razor claws digging in,
I can't take it anymore!

Fall, fall, fall, fall,
Bang! my head . . .
I always have this dream,
When I fall out of bed!

Holly Winwood (12)
Lake Middle School, Lake, Isle of Wight

My Dream

I want to go to Jamaica,
Feel the golden sand between my toes,
See all the people laid in rows.
I want to feel the tropical breeze,
And hear the wind rustling through the trees.
I want to hear the steel drums play,
Until the very end of day,
Go diving in a coral reef
And see the world from underneath.
See the dolphins play and splash,
Tip the waiters with some cash,
Be anything I want to be,
Do anything the world can see.
Sleeping under the starry sky,
I watch the birds as they fly
And as the morning comes today,
I think about it while I lay.
To wish upon the next star I see,
To wish you'll share this moment with me.
Someday I wish I'll end up here,
But till then I'm nowhere near.
This place is where I want to go,
Where there's no thunder, lightning or snow.
This is where I want to go.
I want to go to Jamaica.

Lauren Newland (12)
Lake Middle School, Lake, Isle of Wight

Planet Earth

Don't be so bitter
Just pick up your litter

Planet Earth
Planet Earth

Don't write words on walls
Be taller than tall

Planet Earth
Planet Earth

Recycle, recycle
And use your bicycle

Planet Earth
Planet Earth

All you have to do
All you need to do

Planet Earth
Planet Earth

Save water
Be a walker

Planet Earth
Planet Earth.

Georgia Bennett (12)
Lake Middle School, Lake, Isle of Wight

Mad Dreams

Dreams are odd, curious things,
They infest your brain and make you think things,
Some are good, some are bad,
Some can be achieved, some are mad,
But no matter how mad they are,
Following your dreams is not mad at all.

Tom Carter (13)
Lake Middle School, Lake, Isle of Wight

I Have A Dream

I have a dream,
The world will change,
No more violence,
No more shame,
No more hunger,
No more pain,
No more cruelty,
No more discrimination,
No more racism,
No more war,
I have a dream,
The world will change.

More tolerance,
More peace,
More equality,
More sharing,
More helpfulness,
More ambition,
More desire,
I have a dream,
The world will change,
I will change the world,
We will change the world.

Donna Grady (13)
Lake Middle School, Lake, Isle of Wight

Save The World

The world is full of animals waiting to be saved
Being killed by predatory people every day
Children being bullied or even abused, too scared to tell
Someone hoping it will just go away
Rainforests dying a bit at a time
So come on everyone, fix it and do your bit!

Louise Herbert (12)
Lake Middle School, Lake, Isle of Wight

Dream Cars

Ascari, Ferrari, Maserati,
Lamborghini, Bugatti, Pagani,
I like the DB9,
The Evo X is fine,
Beastly V8,
V12s are great,
The Aston One-77,
Can send you to heaven,
Aston, Lotus, Jaguar,
TVR,
Top Gear,
This Stig,
Some say . . .
He thinks the credit crunch is a cereal
And his first name really is *The*
And that his cousin is the Michelin Man,
He drives quicker than Lewis Hamilton,
All his mind thinks is,
Torque, power, brake,
He is paid to race,
He is the best,
I wish I were him,
That is my dream.

Haydn Nigh (12)
Lake Middle School, Lake, Isle of Wight

I Have A Dream

A mazing attitude

D reams to be revealed
R ealising ambitions
E verybody has a right
A ll are equal
M emories to make and memories to live.

Aaron James (13)
Lake Middle School, Lake, Isle of Wight

My Dream

My name up in lights
On this, oh sweet night
Hollywood waits for me
Gonna be a celebrity

Actress, that's me
Flash, flash
Red carpet
Fan clubs
Give the people who they love

Well, a girl can dream
I like being
Part of a team
On set costumes are great

Movies I'm in
'Wild Child', 'HSM'
'Mamma Mia'
A whirlwind of movies
Singing

Dreams show
Who we really are
So embrace them.

Amber Khan (13)
Lake Middle School, Lake, Isle of Wight

My Dream

A chance to change the world
R ealising artistic patterns
T elling stories through art
I ncredible pictures
S pectacular drawings
T actical paintings
S uccess in all that I do.

Elliott Edgington & Shaun Rockall (13)
Lake Middle School, Lake, Isle of Wight

This World

Can we stop this now?
The world full of rubbish
Can we stop this now?
We can!
What about rubbish?
What about the world?
Can we do this now?
Clean up this world!
Can you stop it now?

I want this to stop now!
All the rubbish surrounding this world
Any more will kill off this world.

Can this just stop?
All the rubbish in the world
And in the streets.
Come on, clean up now!

Can we do this now
Or will we watch the life all die?
Can you just *stop?*
Think about what you are doing now!

Just stop now!

Amy Clarke (11)
Lake Middle School, Lake, Isle of Wight

Abuse

A ct quick, say no to abuse
B lood runs down the victim's face
U nder abuse you want to say something but you can't
S aying something may cause you pain, seeing my kids smile
  makes me overwhelmed
E ventually it stops, they're sent down for what they've done,
  now you can live a special life.

Holly Beckley (11)
Lake Middle School, Lake, Isle of Wight

Forever Friends

The world is not as you think,
Not fluffy or pink,
People live and people die,
And sometimes I wonder why,
We have to be enemies,
Instead of a colony of happy bees,
All of us in a friendship circle,
No one black, blue or purple,
No more horrid fights,
Everyone respecting each other's rights,
No more sadness, only joy,
Like a little boy with a brand new toy,
United as one being,
Not a soul fleeing,
Peace, love and friendship,
Where the boat won't tip,
It's my dream,
To shine a torch beam,
On everyone that is alone or sad,
And add them to the circle and make them glad,
Every little girl and lad,
Together, forever in the circle.

Phoebe Hein (12)
Lake Middle School, Lake, Isle of Wight

Smoking

S ave a life, help a life
M ove on
O pen your eyes
K illing, think about your decision
I should stop smoking
N ot easy, but it is worth a try
G o and do something.

Charlie Wright (11)
Lake Middle School, Lake, Isle of Wight

Together

My world is not equal
My world has no grace
Together we could make it
A better place

Should we stop trying?
Should we give up?
Or should we stick to it?
Without fail, with luck

My world is not equal
My world has no grace
Together we could make it
A better place

So now we'll start again
Rising above
Green meadows, red flowers
And don't forget love

My world is not equal
My world has no grace
Together we could make it
A better place.

Sophie Cusworth (12)
Lake Middle School, Lake, Isle of Wight

The World

The world is full of sunshine
The world is full of brightness
The world is fabulous to be in
The world is full of some bad things
But most of all it is full of goodness
The world is a beautiful place to live in
The world is peaceful and full of love
It is a very kind place to live in.

Danielle Taylor (12)
Lake Middle School, Lake, Isle of Wight

Our Dreams

Dreams are wonderful things,
Even if you can't reach them.
You might want to be an astronaut,
Fly to space, see the moon and stars.
You might want to be a barber,
Cut, curl and colour hair.
You might want to be a zookeeper,
Look after, care for and feed the animals.
You might want to be a footballer,
Dribble, kick and score goals.
You might want to be a trapeze artist,
Swing, fly and jump in the air.
You might want to be an accountant,
Work with a pen and paper all day long.
You might want to be a pop star,
Sing high and low for each note.
You might want to be a maintenance man,
Make, fix and replace things.
You might want to be a fireman,
Use hoses and put out fires.

I know what I want to be, do you?

Katie Davis (13)
Lake Middle School, Lake, Isle of Wight

My Mum Is The Best

My mum is so nice,
She cooks my favourite, rice.
She cooks, cleans and works 24/7,
I wish my mum will never go to Heaven.
My mum is sympathetic when I'm down,
She gets me gifts, even my own crown.
My mum has a vase I cannot touch,
But I love my mum, so much, so much.

Toby Wilcock (13)
Lake Middle School, Lake, Isle of Wight

Stop Bullying

Have you ever heard the cries
Of people telling lies?
People who are threatened
By bullies that won't forget them?

In work or school, everywhere they go,
They know,
Every corner they turn,
They know
That someone is waiting for them
To say words like 'nerds'.
If they yell, 'stop', they just get more knocked.
They get pushed in the dirt,
Every day they get more hurt.

Every hour it makes them melt,
They just want someone to help,
To see how they felt.
But you can stop it,
Just tell someone, I am sure it will stop.
Let your voice be heard,
Stop bullies!

Meg Harper (11)
Lake Middle School, Lake, Isle of Wight

Bullies

Bullies - stick up to them
Bullies - don't worry
Bullies - talk to them

Bullies - need help
Bullies - hit people because they can't express themselves
through words

Bullies - think they are really hard
Bullies - *help them!*

Samuel Durrant (12)
Lake Middle School, Lake, Isle of Wight

Dreams!

Dreams are many things,
Like pigs that have wings,
Ones that can fly,
But my dreams are a little different.

I imagine chocolate-covered worlds
And money that grows on trees,
I imagine saving the pretty honeybees,
Figure skating all my life and spinning those twisty twirls.

Bringing people back to life would be so amazing,
Every year would be white at Christmas,
But think of all those poor, cold donkeys grazing,
And every day would be white on my ice.

My house would be as big as a castle,
The swimming pool as big as a field,
Saving animals that are nearly extinct,
Sometimes I wish some of those animals didn't stink.

So here I end my poem by saying,
Nothing is always what it seems,
But these are just my crazy dreams.

Jodie Hemming (13)
Lake Middle School, Lake, Isle of Wight

Smoking

S ave my people who smoke because their lives are at risk
M y life, really! My life is at risk!
O pen the door to stop smoking
K illing, does it really kill you?
I t does and I nearly died, so I stopped
N ever, I think I will stop smoking if it causes you to die
G o, go, open your lungs to see what's inside you
and doctor, see what's in there as well.
Stop! smoking.

Sam Lancey (11)
Lake Middle School, Lake, Isle of Wight

My Dream As A Marine Biologist

Crashing, roaring waves,
Thunder on the beach; they beat
My future begins.

Diving with dolphins,
I see beyond the sea bed
My future begins.

Exotic clownfish,
Tickle me as I swim by
My future begins.

Sharks search for their prey,
I watch them secretively
My future begins.

Beautiful conch shells,
Lay half buried in the sand
My future begins.

On the beach I rest,
Thinking of what to do next
My future is *now*.

Chloe Bird (12)
Lake Middle School, Lake, Isle of Wight

Why Do People Smoke?

It damages your body
Fills up your lungs
Once you start, you keep on going
It's time for you to drop your cigarette
Then you won't regret it.

Do you know what's in it?
What's making your heart pound?
Have you found the right solution
To start or *stop* all round?

Anna Cole (11)
Lake Middle School, Lake, Isle of Wight

My World

I want a world with a chocolate land,
We're all together hand-in-hand.
I want to see and hear a sight,
Where not a man or woman fight.
I wish for a world which has no rules
And we'd all dance around like stupid fools!
I wish the world would look and see
And not watch people run and flee.
If my world could be as I dream,
The sea would be jelly and clouds would be cream.
If my world could be as I dream,
You wouldn't hear the children scream.
Hopefully there will be people like me,
Who wonder how nice the world could be.
Hopefully, there will be no more wars,
No more fighting, no more laws.
If you have a dream like me,
Open your eyes and then soon see
That the world should be like this
And watch the people hug and kiss.

Millie Graham (11)
Lake Middle School, Lake, Isle of Wight

Carpenter

C reate a masterpiece
A ppreciate the grain
R eact to changes in the wood
P atience
E ncourage others
N ew furniture to treasure
T reat the timber carefully
E xcellent
R etry if you fail.

Billy Rose (12)
Lake Middle School, Lake, Isle of Wight

The Days Are Blue

She says *'Oi!'*
I say, *'What?'*
She says, *'Smack!'*
But I'm just a little tot!

She is there day and night.
She is only nice when she wants a fight!
She tells me to give her this and that,
But I really want to give her a *smack!*

It's a never-ending tale . . .
She says *'Oi!'*
I say, *'What?'*
She says, *'Smack!'*
But she forgets I'm just a little tot!

She never says, *'Hi!*
She always says, *'Smack!'*
But I say, *'What?'*
I'm just a little tot!

You can say *stop* to bullies!

Courtney Sandison (13)
Lake Middle School, Lake, Isle of Wight

The World

The world is a beautiful place
The world is full of sunshine
The world is full of people
The world is full of animals
The world is full of war
The world is full of love
The world is full of hate
The world is full of plants
The world is our home
The world is a beautiful place.

Paige Arnold (11)
Lake Middle School, Lake, Isle of Wight

A Dream That Won't Come Soon!

To my world,
So sweet and dear,
You have finally created a tear,
It is streaming down my face!

You are beautiful,
From top to bottom!
Roses as red as blazing heat!
Trees as high as the sky!
Bumblebees that always *buzz* by!

I have a dream
A world *without* violence
Or
Pollution!

We are the human race,
We are the disgrace!
Selfishly,
We have ruined
This luxurious place!

Kieran Calvert (12)
Lake Middle School, Lake, Isle of Wight

Environment

Help the environment
Help the animals
Help the people
Help the trees and plants
Help everyone live in peace
Help the world.

Help save the planet
And make it a happier place for everyone.
So stand up and do something about it
And don't let it fly past you!

Clara Murphy (11)
Lake Middle School, Lake, Isle of Wight

Lost Forever

All was silent,
All was calm.

I walked into nothingness,
I searched for you.

Your face was untouched,
Your eyes dazzling, but not yours.

What happened to your scarred face?
What happened to your unmendable features?

You weren't as you were last time we met,
You weren't the sister I remember and love.

I didn't notice your changes at first,
I just ran, ran into your arms.

All was silent,
All was calm.

I was in my bed,
I was alone once again.

Chelsea Simpson (13)
Lake Middle School, Lake, Isle of Wight

Do You Do Drugs?

Don't do drugs
Drugs are dangerous
Drugs are death traps
Drugs are a dart to the brain

Turn it around
Talk to friends
Be strong
Talk to Frank

Don't be foolish
Don't do drugs.

Kane Fox (12)
Lake Middle School, Lake, Isle of Wight

My Dream World

I dreamed the world was how I wanted it to be,
I dreamed it always snowed,
Seeing the world in glinting white,
To see snow as tall as mountains and to feel the snow crunch,
I dreamed I could have a massive snowball fight,
With snow being fired like cannons.

I dreamed I had my own rocket with flaring colours,
To be able to fly in a matter of seconds to the moon,
I dreamed we were on the moon, to touch the grey surface,
To feel its rough texture and gaze on a breathtaking object,
Earth!

I dreamed the world was made of chocolate,
To walk on the brown, chocolate street,
Munch on the mouth-watering chocolate lamp post,
And drink from breathtaking chocolate waterfalls.
I have
Dreamed.

Joshua Collings (13)
Lake Middle School, Lake, Isle of Wight

War

War, should it stop?
War is a bore
So don't want more.
War is stupid
It's not loved by Cupid.
Don't like war
It will make you sore.
If you like war
Then you've walked into a door.
So do you hate war
Or do you want more?

Connor Gray (12)
Lake Middle School, Lake, Isle of Wight

Why Is It Me?

Why is it me
That gets abused for being myself?
Has to give up seats on a bus?
Can't go to school like the others?
Is separated from the rest?
Is beaten for what I want?
Is used as a slave?
Isn't important?
Is killed for the colour of my skin?
It's not my fault, it's just who I am.

I sometimes sit and cry
Wondering, *will it ever go away?*
Thinking, is anyone helping me or
Is it me against the world?

I found out today there are people helping
It might not be long now
Before I am treated the same.

Blythe Ely (12)
Lake Middle School, Lake, Isle of Wight

What About?

What about all the people's dreams?
What about people being mugged?
What about the killing?
What about all of our joys?
What about crying whales?
What about the common man?
Can't we set him free?
What about the children dying?
Can't you hear them crying?
Where did we go wrong?
Someone tell me.

Josh Clark (12)
Lake Middle School, Lake, Isle of Wight

My Dreams

I have a dream,
To be the best,
To see the world
And stop the worst.

I have a dream,
To stop pollution,
To stop killing
And to stop weapons.

I have a dream,
Where I've been seen
And given lots of money
And a great big house.

I have a dream,
Where my loved ones that remain, stay
And the ones that don't remain
Come back to me again.

Sophie Knight (13)
Lake Middle School, Lake, Isle of Wight

Billy And The Bully

A kid called Billy
Got hit by a bully
Every day after school.
One day in a pool
Billy saw the bully cry
It turned out he got hit by a pie.

The next day, walking home
The bully came running with an ice cream cone
Saying, 'Why were you laughing at me in the pool?'
Billy replied by saying, 'Why's laughing so uncool?'
The bully turned and stuck the ice cream in his face
So Billy said, 'That's a big disgrace.'

Ben Wraxton (11)
Lake Middle School, Lake, Isle of Wight

I Have A Dream 2009 - British Isles

Acid Tears

My tears are powerful acid
They burn through my skin
I try not to cry
But it hurts.

We are all different
From what I can see
But anger and aggression
Affects me.

We all have a heart
We all have eyes
Why is being different
Such a surprise?

My tears are powerful acid
They burn through my skin
I try not to cry
But it hurts.

Katie Lear (12)
Lake Middle School, Lake, Isle of Wight

The Guys In Afghanistan

The guys in Afghanistan shouldn't be out there,
Will the government ever listen, it isn't really fair.
Men are being killed by explosions and the rest,
That's just the Taliban, they think they are the best.

Young men in the battlefield shouting, 'Go, go, go!'
But the courage isn't there, will it ever show?
Power is the thing, everybody knows
We will be pulled out of there when the power goes.
Can we take a break, get into the shade?
The thing is, if we do, we will start to fade.
Bravery is the key, everyone can see,
When we start to listen, peace will start to be.

Harry Lovett (12)
Lake Middle School, Lake, Isle of Wight

Fire Earth

What about the fish
That live in the sea?
What about the sharks
The kings of the sea?

Fire on the Earth
Sun beating down
Fire across the fields
Men falling down

Time to stop the bullets
Together joining hands
Make up the Earth
Before it's out of hand

Drop your evil spirit
Leave it behind
Go make friends
And live normal kind.

Aaron Jacobs (11)
Lake Middle School, Lake, Isle of Wight

I Have A Dream

I ntelligence for games

H aving to carry on
A mbition
V ivid
E xperimenting

A chance to change the world

D reams to make a game
R unning the premiere
E xciting new games
A im to be the best
M aster of all.

Ben Taplin (13)
Lake Middle School, Lake, Isle of Wight

My Hero Mum

My hero is with me every
Step of the way,
She makes me dinner
And makes me feel safe.
I'd just like to say I love her a lot.

This hero of mine
Is just my mum,
She's kind and loving,
She understands me.
We go out shopping just for me.

When I am ill she brings me soup
And helps me fall
Asleep at night.

My mum is one of a kind,
That's why she's my hero,
Forever and for evermore.

Joanna Hewison (13)
Lake Middle School, Lake, Isle of Wight

I Have A Dream

I   can do anything I want to do

H ave a horse and be a mounted cop
A mounted cop will be a good job
V ery big responsibility to have
E very day I have to get up early

A nd prepare myself for the day ahead

D ay by day, days go on
R ecently we have stopped every riot
E ven though I have never been hurt in a riot
A nd it was a really good job, I will not forget
M y dream is the best.

Luke Sheard (13)
Lake Middle School, Lake, Isle of Wight

Pink And Purple, Orange And Blue

Pink and purple, orange and blue
I'm quite different compared to you
I'm a boy and you're a girl
My hair's straight and you have curls

Discrimination is wrong
Segregation is wrong
But one thing's for sure
We all belong

My eyes are blue and yours are green
I like the sand and you like the sea
Your skin's dark and my skin's light
I'm quite silly and you're so bright

Pink and purple, orange and blue
I'm quite different compared to you
I'm a boy and you're a girl
But all together we will have a better world.

Jack Pattinson (13)
Lake Middle School, Lake, Isle of Wight

I Have A Dream

I have a dream to be a footballer

H ope to achieve my goal
A lways try my hardest
V ying for places
E very second on the pitch counts

A mazing attitude

D o everything I can do
R each my targets
E verything is about football
A nything you want to be, you can be
M aking a difference.

Dan Tibbett (12)
Lake Middle School, Lake, Isle of Wight

Bullying

Sitting on the bench,
Alone in school,
No friends to play with,
No friends at all.

Bullies coming over,
You hide behind the bench,
All you can see is his fists,
As they begin to clench.

Confused as to what they'll do,
You don't make a sound,
You cannot resist,
But to take a peek around.

Caught a glimpse at where I am,
Kicks and punches leave me afraid,
Toss and turn as I lie in bed,
Who knows, tomorrow will I be dead?

Jasmine Watt (11)
Lake Middle School, Lake, Isle of Wight

I Have A Dream

I have a dream

H ope to travel the world
A ustralia would be a good start
V isiting family and friends
E ating different foods

A cross the open seas

D rifting on the waves
R owers row by
E agles circle the sun
A dmiring the open waters and the dolphins
M aking my way around the glorious world.

Danii Wells (12)
Lake Middle School, Lake, Isle of Wight

My Dream World

My dream world is,
A three-storey home,
Sparkling accessories
And a pink, fluffy phone.

My dream world is,
A garden swimming pool,
With ocean-like blue water,
Splashing in the wind.

My dream world is,
An icy floor in my living room,
My secret icy tomb,
The place I feel alive.

My dream world is,
All this and more,
Holiday homes and money trees,
These are my dreams.

Hannah Barfoot (13)
Lake Middle School, Lake, Isle of Wight

Racism

I believe that we are all one world
And no one should be looked at
By the colour of their skin
But the person inside them
No matter who you are
Or what you are
You have feelings
We should all live a dream life
The one we wish, wonder and dream
So I believe we should give
Racism the red card
Because we all have rights.

Lewis Wood (11)
Lake Middle School, Lake, Isle of Wight

The War Poem

I know that a war is on in Afghanistan,
But we shall stand tall at the end of all this.
If we stay on the defence our days are surely numbered,
That is why we have to take this fight to the Taliban.
We shall get vengeance on the massacre of the London bombing in 2005,
Buses were destroyed, trains as well.
Sure, it wasn't as bad as 9/11 in America,
But it was still a disaster.
Could you imagine how the relatives of the attack are feeling?
How would you feel if your friends or family died on a bus or train?
Our soldiers are falling one by one
And we shall go to their homes.
To succeed we have to invade Afghanistan.
Now some people won't be so sure about this.
Do you want them to invade
And shall we win this war whatever the cost?

Ryan Heelan (12)
Lake Middle School, Lake, Isle of Wight

My Hero

My hero is amazing,
He always helps me in troubled or sad times,
But the good thing is, he never gets mad,
Even when I'm bad.
I am talking about my super cool dad,
He takes me for a curry and then to the club,
It helps me get over the bad week.
We're together and happy,
Even if we don't speak.
He's always full of laughter, joy and love.
He makes me very happy and is full of love.
There, I've told you all about my superhero.

Daniel Barlow (12)
Lake Middle School, Lake, Isle of Wight

I Have A Dream

I wish I could fly
My wings can flap
And I occasionally cry
Going to clap
I want people to rely on
Nobody will do the slap
Everyone can be my friend.

The things I like are cool
Hope to do things right
Anything else I don't really like wool
The dark is OK but I need light.

Dark is sometimes scary
Rhyming is a good thing
Everybody can get lairy
And I can hear the bells go *ding*
Many people are generous.

Leah Simpson (12)
Lake Middle School, Lake, Isle of Wight

The Homeless

What about the homeless
When you're led in bed
Do you think it's funny
When they don't have any money?

What about the homeless
When you play on your Wii
Do you think it's funny
When they don't have any money?

What about the homeless
Will it ever stop?
Let's all join together
And help it all to stop.

Kyle Jones (11)
Lake Middle School, Lake, Isle of Wight

I Have A Dream

I have a dream that I can fly,
Up in the sky like the birds so high,
I can shoot laser beams,
As amazing as it seems,
I have a dream.

I have a dream,
To wear stylish superhero suits,
Accessorised with my own rocket boots.
The suit will be bullet-proof,
Strong enough to zoom me out the roof.
I have a dream.

I have a dream to lift up cars,
With my super strong arms I can break metal bars.
I will keep all the villains at bay,
I will be the one who saves you every day.
I have a dream!

Ashleigh Jones (12)
Lake Middle School, Lake, Isle of Wight

Bullying

Bullies do name-calling,
Bullies are hurtful,
Bullies are mischievous,
Bullies are horrible.

Bullies upset people,
Bullies are bad,
Bullies are mean
And make people sad.

So keep control,
So nothing gets worse
And stick your head out
And tell someone first.

Hayley Evans (11)
Lake Middle School, Lake, Isle of Wight

I Have Dreams

I have many dreams
Dreams that are for the whole world
Yes, this nasty world

One of my dreams
Is that wars will not occur
Everybody calm

I have many dreams
Dreams for a peaceful new world
Everyone happy

Forever I dream
For people to be equal
All colours and race

I have many dreams
I hope and dream one day
My dreams will come true.

Charlotte Everist (12)
Lake Middle School, Lake, Isle of Wight

Just Stand Up To Them

Sitting on the swing
No people to play with
Nothing to do at all
His parents think he is fine
They ask him why he has bruises
When he comes home from school
He just says he fell over
But it is much, much more
The bullies used to be his friends
Until they turned on him
They met other people
And said they didn't even know him
But now he is popular and they have nothing.

Jack Broadhead (12)
Lake Middle School, Lake, Isle of Wight

I Have A Dream

I have a dream,
That someday
I will be who I want to be,
I will get the grades I need.

I have a dream,
That everyone in the world can be
Who they want to be,
They can go to school and get those grades.

I have a dream,
That people who might be successful
Will be successful.

I have a dream,
That someday we can all be who we want to be,
That I could change the world
And make it a better place.

Amber Cook (12)
Lake Middle School, Lake, Isle of Wight

Bullying Has Got To Go!

Bullying is no good,
Sitting in the corner
With your head under your hood.

Too scared to show your face.
Too scared to face the world,
Bullying is a disgrace!

Every day just before class,
The bullies take my money,
And they just find it funny.

At the end of the day, no kicks or punches,
So that means no more horrible break times
Or dreadful lunches.

Lauren Sparrow (12)
Lake Middle School, Lake, Isle of Wight

I Had A Dream

I had a dream that I would be . . .
President
Peacemaker
A rock star
An astronaut
A superhero
A fireman
A doctor
A footballer
An Olympic star
An F1 racer
A detective
In the army
Part of a team
Now look at me
I followed my dream.

Kyle Chessell (12)
Lake Middle School, Lake, Isle of Wight

Bullying

They call us thick,
They steal our lunch,
All they do is kick
And they just punch.

They hurt me with words,
They push me with force,
They punch all the nerds
Because they are the source.

They're always picking
And calling us freaks,
They also keep flicking
And kicking the geeks.

Matthew Gibbon (11)
Lake Middle School, Lake, Isle of Wight

Dreams Are A Curious Thing

Dreams are a curious thing,
You can have stories, hopes, and even lives,
But this one was about a world,
A world that was far away from our own,
Earth!
It is a world so different that the real world seems
Impossible to its inhabitants.
That only occurs in a dream,
Dreams are a curious thing.

This world has no pollution,
The air is clean and the sky is blue,
And money has no meaning.
Space is no longer a mystery and starships
Fly across the sky.
Dreams are a curious thing.

Mark Birch (13)
Lake Middle School, Lake, Isle of Wight

The World Is . . .

The world is a football pitch,
Where everyone plays football,
Through the day and through the night,
Everyone plays football.

The world is a land of chocolate,
Where everyone eats chocolate,
Through the day and through the night,
Everyone eats chocolate.

The world is a playground,
Where everyone plays games,
Through the day and through the night,
Everyone plays games.

The world is whatever you want it to be!

Nathan McCarthy (12)
Lake Middle School, Lake, Isle of Wight

I Have A Dream

To help people in court,
To win a battle,
Against all the odds,
So they feel happy once more.

To know that,
I have done a good deed,
And tried my best,
To fight for a person.

To know that,
People trust me,
And they know I can help them.

I will try my hardest,
So I can help everybody,
And to serve the public.

Zoë Lane (11)
Lake Middle School, Lake, Isle of Wight

A Dream World

A dream world is
A sweet world
A happy world
No guns, no bullies

A dream world is
A newborn baby
A small bird
No guns, no bullies

A dream world is
The smell of fresh grass
The smell of a rose
No guns, no bullies.

Katherine Turner (12)
Lake Middle School, Lake, Isle of Wight

Quit It

I'm not scared of the bullies at school
I'm not scared of the bullies trying to drown me in the swimming pool

I'm not scared of the people that live down my street
I'm not scared of my mum's violent boyfriend, Pete

I'm scared my mum might die
Why do I have to lie?

I can't be alone again
You can't leave me with them

Stop smoking
I'm not joking

Give up forever
And we might be able to spend some more time together.

Kimberley Wills (12)
Lake Middle School, Lake, Isle of Wight

Here Comes The Bully

Hiding under the covers,
Too scared to go to school,
You are screaming,
Mum is pleading.

Standing by your locker,
Scattering your books,
Need to run away,
As the bully has approached.

They didn't get me this time,
But Wednesday is always new.

Max Harris (11)
Lake Middle School, Lake, Isle of Wight

Why Should We Remember?

I was told
My great grandad
Was in the RAF
My other grandad was a marine.
I wonder what it was like back then
Fighting an enemy mostly unseen.
I wonder what Heaven is like
I don't actually think there's a Hell,
Cos it's just another word for all the bad stuff
That so many fought against and fell.
If these people did not fight for us
Then we would not be free
And every November the eleventh I thank
The men who fought for freedom,
By wearing a poppy.

Brandon Hanmore (12)
Lake Middle School, Lake, Isle of Wight

Abuse/Peace

A nger, afraid
B ullying, bruises
U nco-operative, unreliable
S obs, sighs
E motions, empathy

P eace, peace
E motions, everlasting
A ffection, attraction
C aring, co-operation
E njoyable, empathy.

Elliott Bell (13)
Lake Middle School, Lake, Isle of Wight

Sunset . . .

Just beyond the sunset
Someone waits for me
Just beyond the sunset
Lies my destiny
Just beyond the sunset
There is a pot of gold
Just beyond the sunset
A legend is told
Just beyond the sunset
I could make a wish
Just beyond the sunset
There is a flying fish
Just beyond the sunset
Behold true love's kiss
Just beyond the sunset . . .

Maddie Hughes (12)
Lake Middle School, Lake, Isle of Wight

Give Up Smoking

You'll get lung cancer
If you carry on
Smoking.
Give up now
Cos I ain't jokin'.
If you need help
Then
Talk to Frank
Because
He's top of the rank.

Sean Skinner (12)
Lake Middle School, Lake, Isle of Wight

Bullying

It doesn't matter what you wear,
Or the colour of your hair,
Because everybody's equal,
Everybody's people so you shouldn't care.

You shouldn't pick on people,
Just because of what they look like,
So that's a form of racism
And racism is un-British.

How would you feel
If your elderly grandma got abuse shouted at her?
How would you feel
If you car got racist comments written on it?
How would you feel?
Just ask yourself that question!

Liam Seymour (12)
Lake Middle School, Lake, Isle of Wight

World Peace

Let's stop war in Iraq,
Bring all the British soldiers back.
The families of the soldiers love them so,
Fighting has brought them down so low.

The wars we've had have been very bad,
Most of the soldiers are just young lads.
So many innocent people have died,
We feel there has been lies.
When they said it would all be better,
We got the wrong sort of letter.

Think how much better the world could be,
Staying best friends, you and me.
People from different cultures walking together,
Can't we stop wars forever and ever?

Charlie Abbott (11)
Lake Middle School, Lake, Isle of Wight

My Dream

I want a world where everyone is equal,
Where you dance and sing with other people
And no one has to play by rules
And everyone enjoys their schools.
There is such a thing as a chocolate island,
Where everyone can see it from the highlands.
I wish that I could be so rich
And buy a car which is ever so quick.
But most of all, I wish, I wish,
That I could meet a rainbow fish.

Ali Hooper (11)
Lake Middle School, Lake, Isle of Wight

Bullied Forever

Bullied every day, bullied every hour,
Can't bear to live another day.
As the day goes by, I'm thinking . . .
Is this going to end?
And all this name-calling and pushing
Is driving me round the bend.
I want to tell someone,
But who do I tell?
Will they ever *stop?*

Howard Brown (11)
Lake Middle School, Lake, Isle of Wight

My Future World

My future world would rock
Everything's so cool,
There are so many things
That are bound to make you drool.

There are hover cars as fast as lightning
Skyscrapers as big as the sky,
Luxury houses with leather inside
And the money never runs dry.

Josh Redford (13)
Lake Middle School, Lake, Isle of Wight

I Have A Dream!

M y dream is to be a professional horse rider
Y ellow sun beaming down on me all year round

D o anything I wanted to
R ealising that nothing is impossible
E nd all war
A nd help people around the world dying of starvation
M ake people in Sudan smile
S ome dreams come true and others do not.

Casey Brook-Henderson (12)
Lake Middle School, Lake, Isle of Wight

Dreams

Dreams are . . .
Objectives or targets,
Dreams are aims,
I have a dream,
A dream which has never been dreamed of before,
Out of my wildest dreams . . .

Riggs Hurrell (13)
Lake Middle School, Lake, Isle of Wight

War/Peace

W ar should stop
A nd global peace should go in place
R eal people don't fight

P lease don't fight
E veryone gets saddened by death in war
A nd can't we get along?
C an't we stop?
E veryone that goes to war dies.

Elias Whittington (11)
Lake Middle School, Lake, Isle of Wight

War And Peace

W hy do we fight?
A t sea, on land, at night
R eal people with real families are being killed.

P lease don't leave young children orphaned
E veryone is saddened by war
A lways people die in war
C arelessness causes war
E ven successful people die in war, so stop war please!

Adam Yates (12)
Lake Middle School, Lake, Isle of Wight

Abuse

I believe that physical abuse should stop
And verbal abuse as well.
Just because someone looks different
Doesn't mean you have to say nasty things about them or be physical.
So just remember that we are all different in one way
But the same in another.

Brandon Wright (11)
Lake Middle School, Lake, Isle of Wight

Say No To Drugs And Smoking!

If you say no,
You will feel less low.
Dealing drugs will make you
Have dodgy doubts about your life.
It's like being locked in a dark wardrobe
And never coming out.
Stop it,
Stop it before it starts.

Jade Goodwin (12)
Lake Middle School, Lake, Isle of Wight

Drugs

Dealing drugs will make you hate yourself
Do something positive and get some help
Dealing drugs is like setting fire to a house
Pour on water and stop the flames
You're killing your children, not only yourself
So why don't you stop yourself
Stop! Don't throw your life away.

Rebecca Greenslade (12)
Lake Middle School, Lake, Isle of Wight

My Dream

W ant to invent everything
 I nvent things that will help people
 S ee things that give inspiration
 H ope all ideas come true
 E verything will be made perfect
 S uccess in all I do.

Joshua Taplin (13)
Lake Middle School, Lake, Isle of Wight

Help

D ealing drugs damages and depresses
R ethink your life!
U se drugs *only* for medicine
G o out and get a life!
S topping drugs is like starting a new life!

Georgia Willshire (11)
Lake Middle School, Lake, Isle of Wight

I Have A Dream

I have a dream for you and me,
That we can live in harmony.
No segregation amongst the nation,
No one better,
Not you or me.

I have a dream for you and me,
A world without any poverty.
Why on Earth should we be crying,
When children all over the world are dying?

I have a dream for you and me,
Peace between all nations, the end of the divide.
Some couldn't care less about war in the world,
How would they feel if the tables were turned?

I have a dream for you and me,
Where all of this is reality.
Where blacks and whites can stand side by side,
Never fearing anything, nothing to hide.
Where poverty, what is that?
Where nations stand united,
Filled with pride.

All of this *can* be reality,
If we work together,
You and me.

Shannen Atkinson (12)
Mossley Hollins High School, Mossley

All About Dreams

I have a dream
But what does that mean?
These dreams, what are they?
Why we have them is impossible to say.
Then why I can never dream to imagine
But can't we dream of anything?

Dreaming is like being in a different world
Some are left unended, their mysteries never to be unfurled
Dreaming is where your imagination has no bounds
From reality to dreaming, ounces turn into pounds.
Dreams mystify us, why do they leave us with questions, we ask?
We also think that they leave us with a job or task.

Most dreams we forget when we are asleep
And the ones that we remember are forgotten as well - very
                                                      few do we keep.
But would those ones be dreams or nightmares?
Or a weird dream, more questions, one too private to share.

What toy helicopter can think, shoot or fly?
What cage goes on forever and goes beyond the sky?
What if you were trapped inside and a cheetah was as well?
Now that dream is almost too scary to tell!
What dragon sculpture makes buildings move around?
And hypnotises with its stare and makes structures fall to the ground?

Nobody likes waking whilst having dreams
A story left half-told raises more questions it seems
It may leave us angry or annoyed, mainly the latter
But then we forget the dream, so why does it matter?
Dream interpretation might make things make more sense
But what the dream meant may have already happened or is in
                                                      present or future tense.

So when I have a dream and wake up at the end or middle
It is most certainly going to leave me with a question or riddle!

Nathan Gittens (13)
Mossley Hollins High School, Mossley

I Have A Dream (And You'd Better Like It)

My eyes are green,
Your eyes are blue,
Why am I standing next to you?

It's wrong, it will end,
I'll end it, because discrimination,
Harms the nation,
It's wrong.

Your hands are black,
My hands are white,
Perhaps our friendship isn't right,
Stupid rules, laws, segregation,
Harms creation,

Your dreams can change the world,
Or end it,
We're not different, we're not,
Black, white, wrong, right,
Don't exit,
Won't exist,

I have my dreams,
I can make them come true,
I can, I will,

My eyes are green,
Your eyes are blue,
I'm glad I'm standing next to you.

My dreams can and will come true,
Because we're the same, same heart,
Same hopes, we deserve to live,
My dreams is as important as yours,
And you know it.

Alice Manning (13)
Mossley Hollins High School, Mossley

I Have A Dream . . .

I have a dream -
That the world is made of chocolate . . .
I have a dream -
That money grows on trees . . .
I have a dream -
That I will have a Lamborghini . . .
I have a dream -
That I can walk on the seas . . .

I have a dream -
That I could swallow a sword . . .
I have a dream -
That the world could be a square . . .
I have a dream -
That I was 6ft tall . . .
I have a dream -
That today's society is fair . . .

I have a dream -
That I live in a shoe . . .
I have a dream -
That I was a gnome . . .
I have a dream -
That I had super powers . . .
I have a dream -
That I was made of foam . . .

I have a dream -
That I can dream . . .

Evan McIlwaine (13)
Mossley Hollins High School, Mossley

I Have A Dream

I have a dream,
That the sun shines every day,
And it shines on children as they play,
Life is perfect, quiet and peaceful,
And yet everybody is meaningful.

I have a dream,
That the world is one,
That every drop of sadness has gone,
United hearts beating together,
It will now as it will forever.

I have a dream,
That no deaths are made,
And that my world will never fade.
The world is free,
Just for you and me.

I have a dream,
That dreams never end,
And happiness is only round the bend.
Only light and no dark,
Here is where I lay my mark.

Here is my last dream,
That everything is as it seems,
I'm going to miss my perfect world,
I have a dream, I have a dream,
Now it's your turn to dream, dream, dream . . .

Chloe Brierley (11)
Mossley Hollins High School, Mossley

I Have A Dream

I have a dream,
Of me,
Of you,
And the freedom of ourselves.

Instead of hiding we will run,
Run free of the chain that binds us,
Run free of the chain that keeps us apart,
We will never stop when we start.

I have a dream,
Of us,
Of being together,
No one can keep us apart.

Rules won't apply to us anymore,
Everything we are told will be forgotten,
Everything we are told isn't needed,
We live by our own words.

So now as I take this knife,
I know I can be with you,
I know I can again see you.
With this knife I can go where you are.

I have a dream,
Of me,
Of you,
And the freedom of ourselves.

Jessica Foreman (14)
Mossley Hollins High School, Mossley

I Had A Dream

I had a dream,
Late one night,
The clock struck twelve,
It was midnight.

The door creaked open,
The figure sighed.
This is the story,
Of how I died . . .

It glided into the middle of the room,
I could see through its transparent skin.
It gave me one last quick chance,
To repent any of my sins.

This couldn't be true,
It must be unreal.
This couldn't be here,
It's so surreal.

That was my last thought,
The thing I couldn't mend.
I can't remember anything at all,
And then that was the end.

If I had only that one last wish,
It would be that my short life didn't have to finish . . .

Hannah Willis (14)
Mossley Hollins High School, Mossley

I Had A Dream

I had a dream that society will not be judged by the colour of their skin,
But what is in their loving heart and who they are.

I had a dream that the gangs on the streets didn't have evil guns,
But large grins on their faces and were full of joy.

I had a dream that the community was not teeming with litter,
But clean, safe and green.

I had a dream that no defenceless animals were abandoned or abused,
But all cared for and loved.

I had a dream that there weren't any unfortunate children who cried
themselves to sleep at night because they are harmed -
But were tucked in a warm bed; with a story each night.

I had a dream that the different countries of the world were all equal,
And were not ranked on their wealth or popularity.

I had a dream that every single human being loved who they wanted to,
Not who they were expected to fall for or what was arranged.

I had a dream that there was no need for the army, air force or navy,
Because the whole wide world were friends; one huge family.

I had a dream that one day people could dream about what they desired,
I had a dream.

Lucy Mansfield (14)
Mossley Hollins High School, Mossley

My Dream

My dream, my dream, my favourite dream,
To know everything, do not have to go to school.
My dream, my dream, my favourite dream,
For immortality to come true.
My dream, my dream, my favourite dream,
For the world to live in harmony.

Callum Leech (12)
Mossley Hollins High School, Mossley

Just A Dream

Waves beating on the sand
There we sit hand-in-hand
Waves crash down
And I look around

The sun begins to set
It seems as though we've just met
But we've known each other for quite a while
The thought of you just makes me smile

We begin to slowly walk
Across the beach, we start to talk
Both our footsteps are so in sync
I'm so nervous I can barely think

You stop and look at me
You're all I can see
You lean in -
It's a perfect scene

Everything goes blurred and I can't see
What's happening? What could this be?
I open my eyes, obviously not what it may seem
Because I've woken up - it was just a dream!

Lauren Bishop (13)
Mossley Hollins High School, Mossley

I Have A Dream

I have a dream
And I know it is true,
I will make it work,
For the sake of me and you.

Imagine not being cared about,
Because of the colour of your skin,
Imagine not being cared about,
Because you were fat or thin.

Imagine being judged,
Because of your wealth,
Imagine being judged,
Because of your health.

My dream is,
To stop the prejudiced people
And if this doesn't happen,
You may as well hang me on a church steeple.

I have a dream,
That boys and girls can mix,
No matter the colour
Of their beautiful skin.

Becky-Leigh Grimes (12)
Mossley Hollins High School, Mossley

I Have A Dream

I have a dream
I have a dream that when I wake up
I won't be judged by how I look
I have a dream that across the nation,
Won't be taken over by discrimination.

I have a dream
I have a dream that mixed black and white
Won't be thought of as an awful sight
I have a dream that hatred is gone
And accept creation for how it is.

I have a dream
I have a dream that friends are true
So we can see hard times through
I have a dream prejudice is bad
Therefore no one will be sad.

I have a dream
I have a dream that we are all the same
And we refuse to be influenced by fame
I have a dream that my dream will come true today
This is the only thing I really pray.

Nia Woodhouse (12)
Mossley Hollins High School, Mossley

I Have A Dream

I have a dream,
That all evil can be vanquished, forever.

I have a dream,
That all poverty can be swept away, forever.

I have a dream,
That we all can forgive and make friends, forever.

I have a dream,
That the world will last, forever.

I have a dream,
That the gift of life will linger, forever.

I have a dream,
That peace will flood the land, forever.

I have a dream,
That pollution will become extinct, forever.

I have a dream,
That one day this could be reality, which lasts forever.

Philip Reynolds (11)
Mossley Hollins High School, Mossley

I Have A Dream

I have a dream there were no wars,
No deaths, no lives destroyed,
Every man could get along
And everyone had somewhere to belong.

I have a dream that people would be friends,
No matter what they look like or where they're from,
Black and white, people could live as one.

I have a dream,
An amazing dream,
That the world could live in peace!

Jennifer Moloney (11)
Mossley Hollins High School, Mossley

I Have A Dream

I have a dream,
That no one's mean,
Me and Jack are the best,
We're a sick team.

Wearin' our trackies,
Wearin' our chains,
Chillin' with our mates,
Black or white, we're the same.

Me and ma mate,
Met at high school,
We can be fools,
We can be cool.

We're mint mates,
We're hot, we sizzle,
We're gettin' bored so
Inabizzle.

Yeah!

Jack Shaw (11) & Daniel Parsons (12)
Mossley Hollins High School, Mossley

I Have A Dream

I have a dream,
That the world was all equal,
No wars to disturb the peace,
No need for countries to fight,
I have a dream.

I have a dream,
That the world will have fresh water,
No one will suffer from famine,
Everyone has a home to live in,
I have a dream.

Emma Lowe
Mossley Hollins High School, Mossley

I Had A Dream . . .

I had a dream that would change the world
I had a dream that would bring justice to the world
I had a dream . . .

I had a dream that would end discrimination
I had a dream that little black boys and little white boys could play together
I had a dream . . .

I had a dream that the fire of oppression would be extinguished by freedom
I had a dream that people would be treated as people
I had a dream . . .

I had a dream that one day people would be judged on their
                                        strength of character
I had a dream that there would be no more vicious racists
I had a dream . . .

I had a dream that changed the world
I had that dream . . .

Today!

Charlie Barker (14)
Mossley Hollins High School, Mossley

I Have A Dream . . .

I have a dream not to let any opportunities pass me by.
I have a dream to make the most of my education.
I want to go to college and university.
If I have a family, I want to support them in the best way I can.
I want to have a good job.
I want to have a nice house.
I want to have enough money to go on holiday once or twice every year.
If I'm good at something, I won't give up,
I will try harder to achieve it.
I have a dream to make my family proud of me in everything I do.

Emily Lamb (14)
Mossley Hollins High School, Mossley

I Have A Dream

D ream away the bad in the world
R acism and discrimination
E ating at nature and the good
A re you daunted? Are you scared?
M aybe we can change the world together

I have a dream that I'm in a bubble
N ow I can't hear or see the trouble
T orture and war everywhere
O nly if we work together, nobody will be in despair

S egregation, pollution, what should we do?
T ogether we can do this and carry on through
O nwards to the devil wall
P ity and anger shall be spread to all
P lease help the world and change
I n the task, fight down the range
N ot taking part will stop the world
G ood or bad, say goodbye to all boys and girls.

Charlotte Laycock (12)
Mossley Hollins High School, Mossley

I Have A Dream

One dream, one person, that's all it takes,
One person to speak out over rivers and lakes.

One dream, one person, that's all it needs,
One person to hear the horrible pleas.

One dream, one person, that's all we want,
One person to help, that's all they want.

One dream, one person, it may come true,
One person to say we all need help.

Alexandra Kenworthy (12)
Mossley Hollins High School, Mossley

I Have A Dream

I have a dream,
I have a dream,
Where life and kindness
Will flow like a stream.

I have a dream,
I have a dream,
Where people will work,
Work well as a team.

I have a dream,
Where no one lives in poverty,
No more kids crying,
No one ever dying.

I have a dream,
I have a dream,
Where others can think like me,
Where we can live in harmony.

Mathilda Jackson-Hall (12)
Mossley Hollins High School, Mossley

I Have A Dream

I have a dream!

H aving all the money in the world
A ctions speak louder than words
V isions of change, fairness, peace
E veryone equal, innocent, no one to blame

A rguments and disagreements, destroyed

D estroy all killers and criminals too!
R espect is what we need
E veryone should feel safe in the world
A very free world, no crime or racism!
M y dream . . . has ended!

Andrew Lawton (14)
Mossley Hollins High School, Mossley

I Have A Dream

I have a dream so hear me out,
To run and dance and scream about,
I have a dream with no deaths,
And to hear a thousand babies' breaths.

I have a dream to live together,
Forever and ever, and ever, and ever,
I have a dream with no sorrow,
I hope you all begin to follow.

I have a dream without any crimes,
And hours of family time,
I have a dream to see Heaven
And eat a thousand citric lemons.

I have a dream to get along,
Won't you all sing along?
I have a dream to stop dumping,
Will you help me change something?

Rachel Gaskell (12)
Mossley Hollins High School, Mossley

I Have A Dream!

I believe I can make a difference

H ope is there, just reach out and grab it
A nyone can make a difference
V ery good or very bad, everyone has a right
E very day and every night all must sleep tight

A nyone can make a difference

D iscrimination is against the law
R acism has to stop
E veryone, black and white
A ll need to stand together
M ay you choose to help me save the world.

Sarah Lamb (11)
Mossley Hollins High School, Mossley

I Have A Dream

I have a dream that the world is amazing,
I have a dream that I isn't blazing,
I have a dream.

I have a dream that everyone gets along,
I have a dream that everyone stands tall and strong,
I have a dream.

I have a dream that everyone is treated the same,
I have a dream that we will live as equals,
I have a dream.

I have a dream we will all stand strong,
I have a dream we will get through this,
I have a dream.

My dream will come true,
If I want it to,
I have a dream.

Adam Carter (11)
Mossley Hollins High School, Mossley

I Have A Dream

I nside a cloud

H eaven is near
A ll is calm
V iolence no more
E arth still beautiful

A ngels gazing

D rifting up high
R egret no more
E verlasting life
A ll is different . . .
M y dream, my world, just me.

Shannon Connaghan (14)
Mossley Hollins High School, Mossley

I Have A Dream

I have a dream that there will be peace,
I have a dream that there will be no more fighting.
I have a dream I will be successful in the future,
I have a dream that everyone will be treated fairly.
I have a dream that racism will be banned,
I have a dream that colour doesn't matter.
I have a dream that my family will stay safe,
I have a dream I will keep people happy.
I have a dream I will keep all my friends,
I have a dream people will be respectful.
I have a dream people will see other people as who they are,
I have a dream that some people don't deserve what they have.
I have a dream that the world will one day be free of litter,
I have a dream that the world will stay clean.
I have a dream I will become who and what I want,
I have a dream that I had a dream.

Amy Pollitt (14)
Mossley Hollins High School, Mossley

I Have A Dream

I have a dream

H aving a dream can change the world
A nd stop racism
V ery beautiful and
E verything deserves to be treated the same

A nd stop poverty

D ive for your dream
R ewards will be great
E nd the bad
A nd save the world
M ove!

Joshua Leah (11)
Mossley Hollins High School, Mossley

I Have A Dream

I have a dream the world is in peace,
No more fighting, no more wars,
I have a dream.

I have a dream everyone will live as one,
No more crime, no more pain,
I have a dream.

I have a dream we won't be judged for our looks,
No more discrimination, no more racism,
I have a dream.

I have a dream we will all be healthy,
No more poverty, no more illness.

I have a dream,
A powerful dream,
Make it come true.

Rachel Hardiman (12)
Mossley Hollins High School, Mossley

I Have A Dream . . . Of Living

I have a dream to live my life to its fullest,
Even though we have lived through the dullest.
Look to the future, don't live in the past,
Just make every day last, and last, and last!

I take challenges and risks, no matter what,
Because I want this dream a lot, a lot.
I will see sights unseen and go everywhere,
Because I've got a dream and I care!

I have a dream,
A wonderful dream,
That will happen for you and me,
So take my hand and I will take you there,
Because I have a dream and I care!

Erin Barnes (12)
Mossley Hollins High School, Mossley

I Have A Dream

I had a dream,
I won a race,
I beat the best
Cos I kept my pace.

If you really try hard,
When you're diving in,
You can get the lead,
Then maybe you'll win.

Try hard on your turns
And push off with your feet really fast,
Cos if you push off slow,
There is a chance you will come last.

I had a dream,
I . . . won . . . a . . . race!

Emily Cassinelli (13)
Mossley Hollins High School, Mossley

I Have A Dream

Imagine being alone - nobody to care for you . . .
I have a dream that one day I will have someone who is there for me.
Imagine having no food, scratching in bins . . .
I have a dream that one day I won't have to find food like a sewer
                                                    rat in an alleyway.
Imagine having nothing to call your own . . .
I have a dream that one day I can own something that I deserve.
Imagine having no fresh water . . .
I have a dream that one day I can refresh myself with a glass of cold water.
Imagine having nowhere to go after a hard day's work . . .
I have a dream that one day I have somewhere to rest in comfort.
Imagination is where my dreams have come to a stop . . .
I hope someone will understand!

I have a dream.

Sarah Lowe (14)
Mossley Hollins High School, Mossley

Their Dreams, My Inspirations

Inspirations such as
Anne Frank
Lived long through war
Wrote a famous diary
She did not make it
But fulfilled her dream

Inspirations such as
Margaret Thatcher
First female prime minister
Shows you can achieve
Any dream

Inspirations such as
Miley Cyrus
Teen pop sensation
At just fifteen
Fulfilled her dream

Inspirations such as
Gok Wan
Fashion designer
Clothes buyer
Made his dream

Inspirations such as
Martin Luther King
Believed in
Integration
Not segregation
His dream is coming true

Inspirations such as
Winston Churchill
Would not give in to the Nazis
Gave hope to Britain
His dream came true

Inspirations such as
Barack Obama
First black president
Proved his dream

Could happen

These people had dreams
Inspirations.

Nicole Darrington (12)
Our Lady's RC High School, Oldham

Stella (Dead Hamster)

Why do people die so painfully?
We will never know,
Some are so young,
One was only 2.

She lived the last days
Making the best of them,
Knowing she would die
So painfully.

Water cancer killed her,
She took tablets every day,
But she showed me how to be proud,
Like she was of her life.

It shows me that we should,
Should be proud like her
And make the best of every day,
Even in our last moments.

I should be strong in my life
And stick up for myself,
Stop going in the corner
And protect myself.

It's a valuable lesson
In our lifetime,
We all must learn it,
To live life strong and proud
And respect our life and others' lives.

Johnathan Hilton
Our Lady's RC High School, Oldham

Bruno

I'm tied to a post,
Afraid and alone,
Don't know where I am,
Or where to call home.

It feels empty and quiet,
And it's getting real dark,
There's no one to save me,
Not even if I bark.

I feel really hungry,
Not eaten in days,
'You've been a naughty dog,'
That's what my owner says.

So as I lie here,
In the cold and the wet,
I realise, I have no home,
And I'm nobody's pet.

As I drift off to sleep,
Hoping it will end,
I hear a soft voice,
Saying, 'Hello there, my friend.'

He strokes me very gently
And lets me lick his hands,
I think he really likes me,
I think he understands.

'Do not be afraid, my friend,'
He whispers in my ear,
'I will take good care of you,
You don't have to fear.'

We set off walking down a road,
Now I'm not afraid,
The old man starts to speak again,
'I think you should be named.

Bruno, yes, that suits you well,'
I bark as I agree,
I love my new owner very much
And I know that he loves me!

Chloe Appleby
Our Lady's RC High School, Oldham

Those Inspirational People

Those inspirational people
They go out and risk their lives
But this we just do not realise
It must take some guts
All those bruises and cuts
Those people are soldiers at war
Those inspirational people
In a time of need
You know they'll be there
For you to turn to
For some love and care
Those people are your family
Those inspirational people
The people who stood up for the rights
For equality of the black and white
Racism is slowly disappearing
Barack Obama, America's first black president I am hearing
Their work is now paying off
Those inspirational people
People who help others far away
Who have no food or drink
And hope they will last another day
There are many of these people
So a round of applause for all those and more
There are loads of inspirational people out there
I have only listed four.

Isabella Smith (12)
Our Lady's RC High School, Oldham

Abused

There must be someone, somehow, somewhere,
To get me out of this nightmare.
My mum's never in,
When she is, I feel safe,
But more often than not,
My dad takes her place.
He beats me,
He treats me
Like I mean nothing.
Are parents meant to be kind and loving?
I can't tell anyone,
How I really broke my leg.
I told the doctor I trapped it in the shed.
He beats me,
He treats me
Like I mean nothing.
Aren't parents meant to be kind and loving?
My mum walks in as he slaps my face,
She starts to cry,
My heart starts to race.
He beats me,
He treats me
Like I mean nothing.
Aren't parents meant to be kind and loving?
Today was the best day of my life!
Caught by my mum,
That horrible man,
Shall pay the price.
Never again shall he make me cry,
No longer shall I look him in the eye.
No beating me,
No treating me
Like I mean nothing.
My mum is the best
And much more loving!

Kristina Taylor
Our Lady's RC High School, Oldham

I Have A Dream . . .

A dream that there will be that day
That day when
I get to see her face
That one I can give her
That one big hug.
You gave me away
In such a good way
We have both moved on
But I know that my dream
Of me and you will one day
Come true.
If I walk into your house
And kids walking round
I will ask, 'Are they my brothers and sisters?'
If so, I want to be their role model
I want to see how they look at me
If they ask if I'm a stranger or a friend
They might be shocked to hear I'm their big sister.
Life has been hard
Hard to know if you're even there
Do you even remember me?
I do not know but I still love you
Even if you don't or you're not there
I'm happy you put me in care
I have a family that love me
Just like you do.

Angie Rodriguez Brady (14)
Our Lady's RC High School, Oldham

Jade Goody

Why do nice people get the worst?
Like Jade Goody.
Cancer - terminal.
She speaks up and warns people,
Lives will be saved thanks to her.

Her wishes have come true,
To marry her true love.
Her kids baptised,
But to die at home will be her last wish.

She has been an inspiration to me,
Welcoming death with open arms,
Carrying on through the pain,
Days passing while she keeps going.

She won't see this world again,
She will be somewhere completely different.
Imagine how her kids feel,
It would feel as though your heart
Has been ripped out and stamped on
Before your eyes.

Why do nice people get the worst?
You still haven't answered my question.
But as they say, life will move on.
But not for Jade,
Her life has ended.

Ashlin Ellis (11)
Our Lady's RC High School, Oldham

Cancer

(In memory of Auntie Pat)

When someone gets cancer
No one understands
What they go through
The chemo and hospital bands
They lose their hair
They find life hard
They sit in their chair
And can only move a yard.

When you're in your hospital bed
Trying to stay strong
Nothing can help it
You have to wait so long
And when that time has come
No one can bear the sun
All their friends and family
Cannot bear their grief.

Now it's time to bury your body
Oh, what can I do?
They cover you in mud
And everyone is feeling blue
RIP.

Katie Dolotko (13)
Our Lady's RC High School, Oldham

I Have A Dream

I have a dream to fly the skies
I have a dream to taste cherry pies
I have a dream to travel the world
I have a dream to find a gold pearl
I have a dream Africa will get wetter
I have a dream my mum will get better.

Laura Marinelli
Our Lady's RC High School, Oldham

That's When You Know . . .

Friends,
Are there for you . . .
You'll know when they're best friends,
Because you'll fall out . . .
But you'll never have a doubt,
That they'll support you . . .
Through anything.
They watch you win . . .
And lose . . .
But they're always there,
On the sideline,
Cheering you on.
They listen to your problems . . .
And try to fix them,
But if they don't,
They try again.
They have a laugh,
And a cheer,
And will always be there for you,
And . . .
That's when you know . . .
They are,
Best friends.

Abigail King (11)
Our Lady's RC High School, Oldham

I Have A Dream

For me I have dreams
Ambitions and goals
To be who I want to be
Please let everyone believe
That all badness ends in sadness
So let us help.

Again I have an ambition
To be a beautician
And to find my dad who I have never seen
This is another dream.

People afar
Wish upon a star
And there I am wishing they come true
Let ill people be better
And have a smile on their face
I have a dream
Which is to be
With my happy family.

Grace Stevenson
Our Lady's RC High School, Oldham

I Have A Dream!

I have a dream to conquer my fears,
I have a dream to dry all my tears,
I have a dream to keep the world clean,
I have a dream to be noticed and be seen,
I have a dream to sing a song,
I have a dream to dance along,
I have a dream to fly in the sky,
I have a dream to eat cherry pie,
I have a dream to look after my niece,
I have a dream to bring world peace!

Sophie Lawton (13)
Our Lady's RC High School, Oldham

Football Match

The players ready for the match,
The keeper's learnt how to catch,
The referee's put on his kit,
Look, he's telling the crowd to sit.
Hot dogs, burgers, all on sale,
Old folk drinking ginger ale,
The commentators are setting up,
Lights, camera, action!

The players are running up,
Ready to win the cup,
End of the game, 0-0 is the score,
England will win, I'm very sure.
It's all down to this last shot,
The keeper's tense and very hot,
Takes the shot and he scores,
That's the game, the whistle blows.

What a game!
Nathan Calland-Storey's my name.

Nathan Calland-Storey (12)
Our Lady's RC High School, Oldham

Untitled

Knives, guns, bombs, war,
Why do we need them, what are they for?
Bullying, racism, sexism too,
What type of world are they creating for you?
Eating disorders, self harm and suicide,
Caused by the evil and lives pushed aside.
Families destroyed and friends on their own,
Left feeling upset, angry and alone.
The bad things we cause should not be allowed,
So make the world better and stand up and be proud.

Elizabeth Earnshaw (13)
Our Lady's RC High School, Oldham

Dreams

As sweet as sugar in the night,
Making all wrongs become right.
Your own little place,
Filling the space,
Thoughts in your head,
While you sleep in bed.

My own personal dreams,
Are unforeseen,
Family and friends,
It not just depends
On fear and hate,
Careers and fate.
In some time,
You won't remember this rhyme.

But love is true,
Not just for you,
But for all over the world,
My dreams will be heard.

Gemma Jackson (15)
Our Lady's RC High School, Oldham

Musicians - Inspiration

Endless hours of scales and arpeggios,
Testing to see how high they can go.
Practising until the notes jumble up,
Playing so fast that they get the hiccups.

Changing notes here and there,
Playing until the pages glare,
Hoping and hoping that the night will come,
Where they can show their talent to everyone.

There's just not enough time in the day,
To practise the pieces they have to play.
The night is now ever so near,
But deep inside they have a big fear.

The night has arrived,
The time has come,
The weight on their shoulders seems like a ton.
But then it's over ever so fast
And then they wish that the moment would last.

Victoria Bacigalupo (12)
Our Lady's RC High School, Oldham

In Her Shoes

Have you ever walked in someone else's shoes?
Seen what they see,
Do what they do,
Involve in their arguments, chilling with friends,
Not having the latest fashion,
Not having the latest trends.

Empathise happiness; share their blues,
Open your heart to those around you,
Talk to someone you wouldn't normally talk to,
Put yourself in their position,
Try on their shoes.

Megan Mitchell (13)
Our Lady's RC High School, Oldham

My Poem

Everyone has a dream,
Yet what does mine mean?
Should I fly up above,
Own a turtle dove?
Wish for world peace,
Act like Mother Teresa?
Become a rap star,
Own a million cars?
No, I know what I want to do,
I want my dream to be true.
I want to have twins
And own up to all my sins.
My dad to think
About how much he drinks,
For my grandma to come back again
And not to go insane.

Amber Parker (13)
Our Lady's RC High School, Oldham

I Have A Dream

I have a dream
That one day I will meet
The player of a football team

I have a dream
That to me
Everything he will mean

I have a dream
That we will get married
And he will cock and clean

I have a dream
That this dream will come true.

Georgie Walker
Our Lady's RC High School, Oldham

Venture Adventure

Flying high with an eagle and a crown
Scraping the clouds in a grey bird
So far away from home
At the call of betters
Their voices riding on waves

The feelings wash over me
I tense my stomach
My shoulders
The poppy fields call
I steal away

The men below look up
Some with fear, others with relief
Others with indifference
Others with awe
Coming to the rescue of people who deserve.

Michael Robson (14)
Our Lady's RC High School, Oldham

Best Friends

My best mates are the best,
They're not like all the rest.
Happy, joyful, great and fun,
They're always there when the day's begun.
Always there when I'm upset,
They comfort me, then up I get.
Play games with me,
Come round for tea
And mess about without a care.
When my hair is a mess,
Or I don't look my best,
My friends are always there.

Molly Greaves (12)
Our Lady's RC High School, Oldham

I Have A Dream 2009 - British Isles

Make Poverty History

Save the planet,
Save the Earth,
But the place we really need to save is
Africa's turf,
From disease-ridden villages,
Both big and small,
AIDS, HIV, let's end them all!
Children are a death sentence,
For mothers to be.
They cut them open,
With dirty knives.
Clean the hospitals,
Let's save their lives!
Make poverty history,
Don't keep it a mystery.

Rebecca Harmer
Our Lady's RC High School, Oldham

Friends

The greatest thing in life is friends
They love you, care for you, but it all depends
A best friend laughs when you fall
Whereas a real friend will help you up to give you a call
They are always there for you when you're sad
But be careful, some things could be bad
A best friend would walk away when you cry
Whereas a real friend would talk with you and never lie
The greatest thing in life is friends
They love you, care for you, but it all depends
So do not worry, you can never lose
I'm just saying be careful who you choose.

Francesca Connolly (12)
Our Lady's RC High School, Oldham

141

I Have A Dream

I have a dream,
That no one will be judged by the colour of their skin.

I have a dream,
That no one should crush another person's dreams.

I have a dream,
That all prisons are empty and no one wants to commit a crime.

I have a dream,
That no one wants war.

I have a dream,
That people will just get on and not argue or be racist.

Elise Robinson (13)
Our Lady's RC High School, Oldham

Dreams

Dreams,
The irony of dreams, is that they are always dreams.
If we complete them, then they become achievements.
The problem with dreams is that they are always the future tense
And we are never acting in the present, always thinking about
                                        the upcoming.
Rather than dreaming, we should be acting,
Rather than wishing, we should be living.

David Kelly (14)
Our Lady's RC High School, Oldham

Rugby

He passed the ball to my right,
Then all of a sudden, that guy gave me a fright!
He jumped on me and gave me a scrum,
I looked at the side of me
And they were there, giving me dirty looks.
I managed to pass the ball to another teammate,
He sprinted along, passing everyone and scored a try.
'Whooo!' he said.

Danny Gilbert (12)
Our Lady's RC High School, Oldham

Help Homeless People

If you ever see a homeless person,
Don't just turn away,
'Cause under all those rags
Could be a jolly good soul,
Just waiting for a person like you.
And if you help them, you don't know,
You could end up with a bodyguard
Or a brand new friend.

Caitlin Shires
Our Lady's RC High School, Oldham

I Had A Dream

I had a dream in the night,
I had a dream to fly a kite.
I had a dream to see my dad,
I had a dream not to be sad.
I had a dream to have world peace,
I had a dream to hold my niece.
I want a dream to live my dream.

Jessica Burnett (12)
Our Lady's RC High School, Oldham

Bullying

I dread going in the playground each day
They wait for me around the corner
I try to escape, but they catch me
Then they tip me upside down and nick my money
When I tell the teachers they never believe me
Then the bullies keep doing it every day
I hate them being nice to other people, but nasty to me
I just wish they would stop it
Because it ruins my life *forever.*

Hannah Lowe
Our Lady's RC High School, Oldham

If I Got Up

If I got up at seven, it wouldn't be natural,
If I got up at eight, it wouldn't be pleasant,
If I got up at nine, I would miss school,
If I got up at ten, it would be fine,
If I got up at eleven, it would be great,
If I got up at 12, it would be lazy,
So when should I get up?

Luis Fay (13)
Our Lady's RC High School, Oldham

I Have A Dream

I have a dream, in which I run,
A man pursues, he has a gun.
I turn to face my enemy,
There's no one else, only me.

I have a dream, in which I dream,
I cannot move, not even scream.
I feel a hand upon my knee,
There's no one else, only me.

I have a dream, in which I fall,
I hit the ground and cannot crawl.
Mere rocks will hear my silent plea,
There's no one else, only me.

I have a dream, in which I drown,
My muffled screams, they make no sound.
I try to swim, but cannot flee,
There's no one else, only me.

I have a dream, in which I soar,
My feet are metres from the floor.
The Earth I now cannot see,
There's no one else, only me.

I have a dream, in which I fly,
A distant star shines in my eye.
My stomach bubbles with great glee,
There's no one else, only me.

I have a dream in which there's you,
Only silence, it's just us two.
It's your sweet smile that sets me free,
There's no one else, only me.

Rebecca Glover (15)
Redland High School, Redland

I Dreamt

I dreamt I was a butterfly,
That flitted across the ocean-blue sky.
Then I dreamt I was a cat,
So fat and fluffy and again, oh so fat.
Then I was a giraffe,
That smelt bad because it never had a bath.
Next I was a dragon, my flame so bright and bold,
When my flame died out, I was oh, so cold.

I dreamt I had a snake,
But he ate my chocolate cream cake.
I dreamt I was a fish,
That jumped so high it flew into my dish.
I dreamt I was a dog,
That chased a flying tree frog.
Then I was a mouse,
Squeaking in a house.

I love to dream of animals,
I'm different every night,
But once I woke up and had a big fright.

There I was in my bed,
I was still a mouse,
Living a life,
With a *wife!*
With 10 other mice as well.

Lauren Hall (11) & Anna Garcia (12)
Redland High School, Redland

I Have A Dream That Occurred A Nightmare

I have a dream
Where cries can't be heard
Where day is as dark as night
My unfortunate dreams leaned
To this uncontrollable sight.

Tigers set wild
Out to the cities
With streets and child
Their hopes turned to pities.

The ocean runs free
And destroys all things
Man-made and natural, trees
Here death never stings
Only joy it brings.

Controlled and powerless
By a man
Cursed if rule-breaking
Not a slap on the hand.

But the sentence to torture
Then to death
This punishment a feature
No faith to be left.

Until my eyes awake to the day
My breathing sensational
The fear burned away
This dream never happened
And so I say I'm lucky
I'm lucky.

Adele Mitchell (13)
St Katherine's School, Bristol

Why Me?

Why do bad things always happen to me?
Why do good things never happen to me?
Why me?
Why me?
Why am I at the back of the class?
Why do I not look as good as the other girls?
Why do the girls laugh at me?
Why do boys not look at me?
Why doesn't anybody talk to me?
Why do I sit on a table on my own?
Why is there something up with me?
Why am I ugly?
Why me?
Why me?
Why are my parents always drunk?
Why do my parents always fight?
Why do I always get locked in my room?
Why does my dad hit me?
Why do I only get fed twice a day?
Why are my clothes what my mum wears?
Why me?
Why me?
Why do I feel like I am all alone?
Why do I feel like the world is balanced on me?
Why couldn't I have nice and loving parents?
Why couldn't I be like the other girls?
Why couldn't I have my own clothes?
Why did it have to be me?
Why am I here?
Why is it me?
Why me?
Why?

Jessica Harper (13)
Sir William Stanier Community High School, Crewe

Do Something Better

Imagine if you were
The world's greatest footballer, or the most famous celebrity;
Or maybe the world's richest person; or even the first person to
land on Mercury,
Nothing happens unless you first dream,
Because there is no magic to success,
Hard work, perseverance and enthusiasm is the answer.
Think.
Not about your fears or frustrations,
But about your hopes and dreams;
Your unfulfilled potential.
Be an optimist, not a pessimist.
In the simpler days, the sky used to be the limit;
But in these modern days, you have to go beyond the sky.
And who knows,
You could be the one to find a cure for cancer,
Or eliminate world hunger,
Or maybe find a cure for AIDS;
Maybe even promote world peace.
Just three words:
Believe, Achieve, Succeed.

Aderayo Folorunso (14)
Sir William Stanier Community High School, Crewe

What If?

Do you love me?
What if I never made any noise?
What if I tidied away all my toys?
What if I were the smartest in my class?
What if I never once smashed a glass?
Would you love me yet?
What if I never whined for money?
What if I never said that you looked funny?
What if I cared for you every day?
What if I never hit the hay?
Would you still not love me?
What if I never met friends in town?
What if I wore every hand-me-down?
What if I missed every school trip?
What if I promised never to pierce my lip?
You still wouldn't love me.
What if I handed you a drink?
What if I didn't pour it down the sink?
Now you love me.
But I can't even look at you.

Charlotte Ayers (13)
Sir William Stanier Community High School, Crewe

Black Or White?

I want a world where if you're black or white,
It's not a problem.

Where a black person can walk down the street
And not have any dirty looks thrown at them or names.

Or worse, when they get bottles chucked at them
Or get hit and killed.

There ain't no problem if you're black, it's only the colour of your skin,
It doesn't change the person inside.

Hollie Andrew (13)
Sir William Stanier Community High School, Crewe

The Love Poem

Life is love
Breaks like a leaf
It flies up and down.

Sometimes we keep it
Sometimes we throw it away
Whatever you do with it
Make sure it doesn't harm you.

From any ages to any colour
It doesn't matter
As long as you love them it doesn't matter.

Feeling nervous is a part of love
Cinema, bowling, you should feel free
Bullying and violence are not a part of love
So they should not be shown to the other sex.

Liam Astbury (12)
Sir William Stanier Community High School, Crewe

Racism

In the world today
There is a lot of racism
So I thought one thing . . .
Why can't we live in harmony
And peace?
Why can't black and white people get along?
It doesn't matter what colour skin we have
It matters what's inside
So I reach out to you
Stop all the racism of the races on the Earth
We should be able to get along
And live in a world without hate and racism.

Leon Robinson & Jack Lightfoot
Sir William Stanier Community High School, Crewe

I Have A Dream/ Vegan For Life

I have a dream for a world of love,
To offer a priceless gift from high above,
To fulfil and mend all the broken hearts,
And bring together fragmented parts,
So all of Man's nature can become a team,
For us all to be one is part of my dream.

From secretive, incredible insects so smart yet so small,
To gigantic giraffes spying above so towering and tall,
If God is the one who created them all,
Why does it give Man pleasure to see them fall?

Science and medicine bring fear from a sacrificing tool,
By causing animals pain is unnecessary and cruel,
Nobody sees the tears that fall down,
From behind the scene when the circus is in town.

I discover and learn more throughout the years,
It sickens me to know their feelings and fears,
With the disloyalty and neglect we pay to them,
How I wish I could share my joy like a princess and a gem.

If I were to be granted one wish in life,
I'd share the love and remove the knife,
So that enemies are regarded as part of the past,
And the future brings happiness that will always last.

Remember the ones who give up their lives for your pleasure,
Hold on to their weeping tears and store them as treasure,
On your perfumed skin and body wrapped in leather,
The amount of affection for them is nothing to measure.

And before I rest my head and go to sleep at night,
I hope and pray we will one day make things right.
But until the day we combined together in a stream,
I'll always believe in the fact that I have a dream.

Rosie Barratt (17)
The Phoenix School, Fulbourn

I Have A Dream 2009 - British Isles

I Have A Dream

Recently I've had an amazing dream,
That one day I can stand up and beam.
Hopefully, all my worries will have gone away,
I hope my life will be like that one day.

I want to visit so many places,
I want to meet lots of new faces.
I want to live trouble free,
I want so much to just be me.

To wake up one morning and just be well,
To be how I was before my health fell.
To do everything I want to do,
To be back with my friends and family too.

I cannot begin to express what's happened to me,
The walls of the hospital is all I see.
Depressed is what you may think I sound,
But through this you don't know how much I've found.

My dreams are becoming reality day by day,
'You're doing so well,' all the nurses say.
Through this the nurses and patients have kept me sane,
I will never slip down this slippery slope again.

Lizzie Hill (14)
The Phoenix School, Fulbourn

Swim, Swim, Swim

Light blue on top
Dark blue deep down
Dive in, be free
Let go of all emotions
Be light as a feather, be free as a bird
Feel the cold damp wrap all round your body
Open your eyes and see all those colours
Floating about beneath and around you
Take in their beauty, their skin, their pattern
Look below
And see the coral reefs
Look deeper
And see the seabed
Is anything there?
Lost treasure or a body perhaps?
Or is there a bed?
Like life after death, does it go on?
Deeper and deeper
Open those eyes and keep exploring
Swim, swim, swim.

Lisa Quick (16)
The Phoenix School, Fulbourn

I Have A Dream

I have a dream that we can finally live in peace,
That differences of opinion can be settled.
Wars will not exist, that threats will be silenced
And the world will be at peace.
I have a dream that we will reach for the stars and grasp its fragile door
That we can discover life and have fun.
I have a dream that death will stop and be locked up forever,
That cries of hunger will be silenced and little ones can go to school.
I have a dream that bombs will no longer be a threat,
That guns and weapons will be gone.
I have a dream that we will conquer with the olive branch and the diplomat,
Not the bayonet and the bullet.
I have a dream that the son will bury the father and not the other
way around.
I have a dream, won't you dream with me?

Jack Smith (12)
Thomas Keeble School, Stroud

What If?

What if there were no wars?
What if there were no floods
And what if the world was a peaceful place?
If the world runs out of its natural resources,
What will we do?
People should be helping each other,
Not fighting each other.
What if racism came to an end?
What if black and white children could hold hands and play?
It's time to make a difference,
I have a dream.
Do you?

Niall Mouat (12)
Ventnor Middle School, Ventnor, Isle of Wight

The Dream For Equality

Many dreams are just dismissed,
Passed on without a thought,
But some dreams stick in our minds,
For equality many have fought.

One of these dreams can change the world,
To make it a better place,
The dream for all to live together,
No matter what their race.

Dreams that are realised can be wonderful,
But some come with sorrow too,
For the dream world we wish for,
The person who must change is you.

Equality is our target,
To become our way of life,
It's our target to live and prosper,
And forget about all our strife.

When a white sits next to a black,
There is no need for bitter dispute,
Peace between our races,
Is the ultimate money for loot.

Equality is paramount,
Equality is our friend,
Equality should stay with us,
Well beyond the end.

It's equality for which we plead,
But do you think it's what we need?

James Dymock (13)
Ventnor Middle School, Ventnor, Isle of Wight

The Dream

What is the question that we all ask?
Why did black people hide behind masks?
There once was a great man,
Who spoke out his dream.
There once was a great man,
Who stopped racism it seemed.
His dream was to bring people out to unite,
To bring people together,
Skin black and of white.
To play in the same parks,
To catch the same bus,
And to stop people arguing,
Stop all the fuss.
His speeches were touching,
His words were all strong,
He was putting a stop to racism,
He was doing no wrong.
So the dream lives on.
He's affected our ways,
But not everyone listens,
To what the great black man says.
There is still some racism, back in our lives,
But we cannot always see it, in front of our eyes.

So *my* dream is this, not big and not small,
But a world that is equal, equal for all.

Cameron Guy (13)
Ventnor Middle School, Ventnor, Isle of Wight

War Is Gore

A world without war,
Imagine what it would be like.
No blood, no gore,
War would be on strike.

Sadly war is not a vision,
It's here, there and everywhere.
It's even shown on television.

Kids don't want to grow up in a fighting country,
They want food, a home and a loving family.
However, others want spilt blood.
Lifeless bodies lie face down in the mud.

War is not for the faint hearted,
Many dear friends slowly departed.
War is not a game,
It's very realistic.

Why do wars start?
Money, oil, land?
These reasons are not very smart.

This poem has no moral,
This poem has no end,
This poem only goes to show,
War is such a shame.

Connah Newton (12)
Ventnor Middle School, Ventnor, Isle of Wight

I Have A Dream 2009 - British Isles

I Want To Be

I want to be,
The best footballer there can be,
To score memorable goals,
Belief and self confidence is definitely the key.

I want to make,
People watch me play,
On TV or at the ground,
Either way, I don't care.

To play for Man United,
To play for England too,
But most of all I want to play
For the people that want me to.

I want to be,
In the spotlight after every game,
Cameras and press focusing on just me,
My life wouldn't be lame.

That's my dream,
To play in the footballers' world,
I wish it would come true,
It would be a brand new life for me.

I want to be!

Chris Delaney (13)
Ventnor Middle School, Ventnor, Isle of Wight

That's My Dream

What if the world was a better place?
What if people were brave enough to speak out loud?
What if every war came to a stop?
What if everyone got on with each other?
That's my dream.

What if there was no such thing as bullying?
What if everyone was treated equally?
What if black and white children were friends?
What if the police didn't have to risk their lives chasing knife crime
                                                              every day?

That's my dream.

What if there were no gangs patrolling the streets?
What if every gun was destroyed?
What if there was more love than hate?
What if everyone had a home?
That's my dream.

Do you have a dream?
So put all weapons down,
Buy instead of steal,
Give money to the poor.

Make your dream come true.

Jake Hitchcock (12)
Ventnor Middle School, Ventnor, Isle of Wight

War No More!

Imagine a world without any war,
When God looked down, a perfect world He saw.
This world of ours was made free of hate,
When the heavens were made and opened their gates.
Imagine a city that is death free,
Where there is no stealing, how wonderful it would be.
If this was our world, then our lives would be great,
But this isn't our world, our world's just full of hate.

This world we live in is full of war,
Where lives are taken for gold people saw.
God looks down and is filled with shame,
When the people of Earth fight for a game.
God has seen our future and so have I,
The nuclear bombs will fall from the sky,
Our land will be ruined; all of the people will die.

The survivors of Earth will struggle for food,
People will go crazy and change their mood.
A horrible death awaits us all,
Unless we let all the hate fall.
Imagine a world without any war,
This vision of mine which others saw.

Luke Pestell (12)
Ventnor Middle School, Ventnor, Isle of Wight

Imagine

Imagine wars coming to an end,
Imagine blacks and whites being friends,
Imagine guns and knives being abolished,
Imagine racism being demolished,
Imagine people not having to go hungry,
Imagine slaves being able to run free,
Imagine floods stopping for good,
Imagine people helping others like they should,
Imagine peace in everyone's heart,
Imagine families not having to part,

This is my dream,
Now what is yours?

Imagine there being no secrets to hide,
Imagine there being no theft or crime,
Imagine everyone getting a second chance,
Imagine being liked, no matter if you like football, math or dance,
Imagine the needy not being so needy,
Imagine the rich not being so greedy,

This is *my* dream,
So what is yours?

Josh Herridge (13)
Ventnor Middle School, Ventnor, Isle of Wight

Future

Future: When your child grows up,
When we make a difference,
When you have a dream,
When you realise what you have done,
What will your future be like?
Future: When you become sad,
When you go mad,
When you regret,
When you disrespect,
When the war is over,
When the white doves fly over.
Future: When we all come together,
When we make peace forever,
When racism is no more,
When we open up the door,
When we let good in and bad out,
When happiness is about,
When no guns are fired,
When forgiveness is hired,
When we all make a difference,
We can all change our future, will you?

Cameron Lyons (12)
Ventnor Middle School, Ventnor, Isle of Wight

I Have A Dream

I have a dream
That war and racism has to stop,
Be kind and friendly to others,
Treat people how you want to be treated back,
Share with other people, they might share with you.
I have a dream,
Be true and not to lie and people will be true to you
And trust you.
Everyone is equal,
Everyone should be treated the same,
Just because you have a different skin colour
Doesn't mean you are treated differently.
I have a dream
In different countries people kill other people
Because of what they believe in,
Like being Catholic or Muslim
Which should stop,
Because everyone should be treated the same in this world
Especially innocent little babies and children
As they don't understand what is going on.

Ahmet Suleyman (12)
Ventnor Middle School, Ventnor, Isle of Wight

I Have A Dream

I am dreaming . . .
Where there are no wars.
Where no one will die
With gunshots in them.
Where wives are not screaming
And children are not lonely.
I am dreaming . . .
Where there is no racism.
Where we are all the same
And no different from each other.
Where no one gets killed because of their skin,
We have different skin and they don't kill us.
So we shouldn't kill them.
I am dreaming . . .
Where there are no drugs or alcohol.
Where people don't have to take them,
Because of peer pressure.
Where no one will be attacked,
Because of drugs.

Caeden Cattell (12)
Ventnor Middle School, Ventnor, Isle of Wight

I Thought

I know the world is sometimes a place of hatred and envy.
I know the world is sometimes a place of pain and suffering.
I know the world is sometimes a place of death and bloodshed.
I know the world is sometimes a place of disagreement.
I know the world is a place where darkness is almost everywhere.

I thought the world was a place of peace and love.
I thought the world was somewhere each person is equal.
I thought the world was a place of no evil.
I thought the sun would shine on all things good.
I thought that would be everything.

Alexander Conrad (13)
Ventnor Middle School, Ventnor, Isle of Wight

His Dream

As good as it seems,
That man had a dream
For all races to stick together,
From the English to the Texans,
The Scottish to the Mexicans,
From obese to as light as a feather.

Then all the races
Started showing their faces
And breaking away from the fear,
From just me and you
To the blacks and the Jews,
Has that dream really come true here?

That was the past,
It all happened so fast,
It was Martin Luther King's speech.
It was inspirational,
Purely sensational,
Anti-racism is something to teach.

Jack Little (12)
Ventnor Middle School, Ventnor, Isle of Wight

Dream

I have a dream that all the trees won't be cut down,
I have a dream that I won't look like a clown,
I have a dream that the guns will stop,
I have a dream that it will be cleaned up with a mop,
I have a dream that the rivers will not overflow,
I have a dream that I can still look out the window,
I have a dream that I can help the poor,
I have a dream that I can help some more,
I have a dream to stop pollution,
I have a dream and this is my solution.

George Atkey (12)
Ventnor Middle School, Ventnor, Isle of Wight

Can The Future Be Saved?

Every day people die,
Every day people cry,
Every day it's the disease,
Who chooses, who deserves peace,
Every day the disease is spread,
Every day the people are scared,
Of losing the lives of their relatives and their own.

Can the future be saved?
Can the future be saved from the deaths of good people?
Can the future be saved from the deaths of bad people?
Can the future be saved by the people who raise money for charity?
Can the future be saved by the people who don't raise money?
Can the future be saved by politicians?
Can the future be saved by music?
Can the future be saved by capitalists?
Doesn't matter who you are, because everyone can do it,
I believe that it's possible, but with some hard work.

James Bott (13)
Ventnor Middle School, Ventnor, Isle of Wight

This Is My Dream

I have a dream in which I hope to stop everything bad happening.

Imagine black people equal to white people.
Imagine no more racism anywhere.
Imagine accepting everyone is different.
Imagine black children are friends with white children.
Imagine no more racism anywhere.

Imagine making everyone be friends.
Imagine making peace in every nation.
Imagine not killing anyone just because of their colour.
Imagine not killing anyone for joining with the wrong gangs.
Imagine life without police, ambulance and fire brigades.

Imagine people stopping knifing anyone.
Imagine guns were only for people with a licence.
Imagine travelling at the speed limit.

This is my dream.

Tom Dawson (13)
Ventnor Middle School, Ventnor, Isle of Wight

No Need

People fight over food
People fight in gangs
People kill for their own satisfaction
People never stop to think
Of poverty or race.

People are rich, they live great
People are poor, they live terribly
What do rich people do with their money?
Whilst poor people wish they could eat.

Countries become an alliance
To help fight other countries
There wouldn't be any need
If we all got along.

There wouldn't be any need
For killing or racism if we all got on.

Tom Redhead (12)
Ventnor Middle School, Ventnor, Isle of Wight

Racism Poem

Why can't black people be treated like us?
They used to not be allowed to catch a bus.
Do they have to be treated this way?
We should really let them have a say.

Normality is what they should live in,
And not be treated like a Biffa bin.
They are no different to us,
Just a different skin colour.
Hand in hand like sisters and brothers.
If we stop racism, then we can all be friends,
No more wars, because they will end.

No more arguments, no more bombs.
Better life for all black people,
Let's chuck racism through the door.
No more fighting, no more war!

Connor Jay Steptoe (13)
Ventnor Middle School, Ventnor, Isle of Wight

I Have A Dream . . .

I have a dream,
One of life, love and unity.
Where the world is free and safe,
Peace and harmony for the community.

We walk among fields of endless money,
Play games in the bewildered sun,
I dream of nothing,
But hope for it all,
My time will come with this rising fall.

I pray for forgiveness,
Against all my sins,
Where the ground opens up and lets me in.
Where the world is at one,
The dreams have begun.

I have a dream,
Where everyone's the same,
The colour of your skin, causes no din.
The colour of your eyes, tells no lies.
We are all equal!

When the war is over
And the damage is done.
The end is in sight but no one has won,
People still remember,
The nightmare's still fresh,
The scars cut hard, deep into the flesh.

I have a dream,
One of life, love and unity.
Where the world is free and safe,
Peace and harmony for the community.

Nikki Carter (15)
Western Study Plus Centre, Grimsby

I Have A Dream . . .

I close my eyes and I'm wandering
Waltzing in silence, piano faded,
I stare at the night unfolded - enclosing me,
Interrupting my dream of escape.

I carry the waltz,
But I waltz to a beat pre-chosen
So I conform to it, and I'm sinking
Into the abyss of music that
Has numbed me in its folds.

I can't stop, the lullaby winds on.
Hypnotic, addictive
By its own recognition,
It can't be helped.

The piano heightens and crescendos to a deafening quarrel,
The invisible piano and pianist crashing,
Together in harmony of an argument,
The piano winning the struggle.

It keeps the beat,
I carry the dance, in my heart
I can't stop,
I'm defying myself not to stop,
To carry on.

Although the inevitable beckons,
The end coming,
Then it stops.
Silence.
But still, a faint whisper
From the night,
A promise,
That my dream will carry on.

Esme Elsden (13)
Withington Girls' School, Manchester

Catching

'I have a dream,' said MLK,
Well I'm sad to say the same.

A crowd of faceless, wingless angels
Falling ever further downward,
Thousand upon thousand,
Million upon million,
Silently screaming through flesh and bone
Into visionless void

And I am the net

I twist and turn
Trying to catch them
To hold them
To save them
The angels

Clawing at air and sobbing through tears
I shut my aching eyes and reach out
Stretching my now bloodless arm
Stretching past possibility
I grasp my waiting hand

On flesh

Pull up! Pull up! Quick, I think,
I've got you and I'm not letting go.
So suddenly had my solitude fled that
I had little room to breathe out.
But I smile to the world
So possible now
As my groundless angel and I reach out together

Into the gulf once again.

Véronique Tamin (16)
Withington Girls' School, Manchester

I Have A Dream

My dreams started along with me,
And I wish my dreams shall not end with me,
I once wished for a shining star,
To guide the travellers from afar,
But as I grew I wished anew,
And then I yearned to comfort you.

The years passed and the world turned,
But my dreams failed so I returned,
Returned to the place buried deep within
Where I searched for ideas held therein,
Then as I dug so deep inside
I felt the urge to travel far and wide.

I roamed the world and I saw such wonders,
Many beautiful things but I began to ponder,
I began to see evil more and more,
And often in the form of deadly wars,
Then my dreams returned again,
And so I wished for an end to pain.

The years have passed and pain has returned,
My dream came back but it is still unheard,
I sink into darkness when I see it is so,
And start to wish for the life I'll never know,
I've spent my life in introspection
But now I just wish that I'd cease to function.

I lost humanity.

Sheanna Patel (13)
Withington Girls' School, Manchester

I Have A Dream 2009 - British Isles

Young Writers Information

We hope you have enjoyed reading this book - and that you will continue to enjoy it in the coming years.

If you like reading and writing poetry drop us a line, or give us a call, and we'll send you a free information pack.

Alternatively if you would like to order further copies of this book or any of our other titles, then please give us a call or log onto our website at www.youngwriters.co.uk

Young Writers Information
Remus House
Coltsfoot Drive
Peterborough
PE2 9JX
(01733) 890066